T0005985

DEFYING DISPLACEMENT

Urban Recomposition and Social War

INSTITUTE FOR ANARCHIST STUDIES
&
AK PRESS

Additional praise for *Defying Displacement*:

"So often gentrification is a process understood in limited terms as a flow of people or the impersonal and inevitable flow of capital. In *Defying Displacement*, Andrew Lee analyzes both in tandem, illuminating how gentrification transforms not only housing markets, but the horizon of possibility for revolt . . . readers will be able to understand this subject with a fresh appreciation of how global struggles past, present, and future are linked by the making and unmaking of cities."
—**Ayesha Siddiqi, editor in chief of *The New Inquiry***

"Andrew deftly outlines the urgency of the housing crisis by centering those that should always be at the crux of the conversation and calls for the radical resistance that displacement deserves."
—**Nicole Cardoza, founder of**
The Anti-Racism Daily

DEFYING DISPLACEMENT

Urban Recomposition and Social War

Andrew Lee

Defying Displacement: Urban Recomposition and Social War
© 2024 Andrew Lee
This edition © AK Press and Institute for Anarchist Studies

This edition © AK Press
ISBN: 978-1-84935-524-7
E-ISBN: 978-1-84935-525-4
Library of Congress Control Number: 2023935625

Institute for Anarchist Studies
PO Box 90454
Portland, OR 97290
https://anarchiststudies.org
info@anarchiststudies.org

AK Press
370 Ryan Ave. #100
Chico, CA 95973
www.akpress.org
akpress@akpress.org

AK Press
33 Tower St.
Edinburgh EH6 7BN
Scotland
www.akuk.com
ak@akedin.demon.co.uk

The above addresses would be delighted to provide you with the latest AK Press
distribution catalog, which features books, pamphlets, zines, and stylish apparel
published and/or distributed by AK Press. Alternatively, visit our websites for the
complete catalog, latest news, and secure ordering.

Cover design by John Yates (stealworks.com)
Printed in the USA on acid-free, recycled paper

"La primera batalla a ganar es dejar participar a la compañera, al compañero y a los hijos en la lucha de la clase trabajadora para que este hogar se convierta en una trinchera infranqueable para el enemigo."

[The first battle to win is to let the partners, female and male, and their children participate in the class struggle so that this home might be converted into an insurmountable trench for the enemy.]

—*Domitila Barrios de Chungara*

Contents

INTRODUCTION

"I love my city more than my own soul."
—*Niccolò Machiavelli*

In May 2018, dozens of squatters launched simultaneous building occupations across Berlin, a "radical intervention against the principle of speculative vacancies" driving up rents.[1] Three days later, protestors shut down a public meeting in the Silicon Valley city of San José, California. For an hour, they shouted down the bureaucrats, nonprofit leaders, and corporate representatives convened to negotiate the details of a Google mega-campus planned for construction on public land in the city core.[2] Community members feared that the arrival of tens of thousands of well-paid tech workers would force an even greater number of residents out of the region or onto the streets. "*San José no se vende,*" they chanted at the suits. San José is not for sale.

City staff called the police and abandoned the room, moving the meeting behind closed doors. One week later, in San Francisco's Mission District, dozens of masked-up protesters in Hazmat suits threw piles of electric scooters into an intersection to blockade tech shuttle buses during the morning commute. "Sweep Tech Not Tents," read the banner that obstructed a bus until its flustered passengers gave up and disembarked. "Silicon Valley nos está matando" read another sign: Silicon Valley is killing us.[3]

On the other side of the country, an anti-gentrification contingent hundreds strong had marched from Temple University to City Hall on International Workers' Day.[4] Formed by two grandmothers, the Stadium Stompers had shut down a town hall meeting about the construction of a football stadium in their North Philadelphia neighborhood earlier that spring.[5] The group demanded that the $130 million earmarked for the off-campus stadium be spent on affordable housing and public education instead.[6]

There was still an open $10,000 bounty on whoever kept shooting a pellet gun at the windows of the private buses that shuttled techies between their San Francisco condos and Silicon Valley campuses.[7] The month before, four people had splashed red paint over artworks—and patrons—inside a white-owned gallery in South Central Los Angeles, a direct action against the influx of white businesses pricing out Black and brown neighbors.[8] The following month would see a Rochester nun lead a protest against the eviction of the residents of a budget hotel.[9] Investors would prevail and eventually sink $16 million to convert the run-down building into a boutique hotel.[10] Berlin would see a "Kick Google Out of the Neighborhood" action coinciding with the beginning of the World Cup.[11] *The Guardian* would report that, after a quarter-century "turning a sardonic pencil on the gentrification of London," artist Adam Dant was finding himself priced out of his east London studio.[12] And a class-action lawsuit would be filed against the city of Washington, DC, alleging that local government was "intentionally trying to lighten black neighborhoods . . . through construction of high density, luxury buildings" for members of the educated "creative class."[13]

We find ourselves amidst struggles, subterranean and open, against forced expulsions from the cities of the world in favor of newer, wealthier, and typically whiter residents. Gentrification sees working-class neighborhoods "invaded by the middle classes"[14] as housing costs rise to levels only more affluent transplants can pay. As neighborhoods transform, potholes might be filled, houses repaired, and supermarkets opened, though these amenities will ultimately be consumed only by those able to afford the inflated cost of living. Neighborhoods long dispossessed and disinvested in are now targeted for reinvestment and replacement by the most powerful institutions in the global order: tech firms and investment banks, universities and politicians, their propagandists and the police.

As the gentrifying district loses Black and brown locals, urban "excitement and diversity" are often joined by suburban amenities and sterility for the benefit of new residents who fancy themselves bohemian—to a point.[15] Capital investment and infrastructure improvements facilitate new luxuries, while increasing police violence and repression ensure the safety and comfort of the newcomers who consume them.[16] Each gentrifier makes the area more palatable for those to follow. Some imagine their new neighborhood as *terra nullius* waiting to be pacified and civilized by the enlightened white professional-class frontiersman, with a video doorbell and histrionic Nextdoor posts in place of a musket and coonskin cap. The result is massive, forced economic displacement until the entire character of the neighborhood is transformed.

For those not forced out, the whole process can be quite lucrative. Economic displacement happens not through oversight or casual cruelty but because a whole range of institutions and individuals profit handsomely. Gentrifiers get appealing amenities in a relatively inexpensive urban environment. Their employers concentrate pools of workers. Property developers and real estate investors make a killing. Politicians watch their tax base grow. The banks that write loans for new businesses and mortgages for new homeowners do nicely, as well. Even nonprofits campaigning against displacement might benefit from the donations of wealthier and guiltier new neighbors.

The only people not liable to benefit are the people who composed the neighborhood in the first place. The residents of post-industrial communities may feel cautiously optimistic that the capital infusions that accompany gentrification will usher their "neighborhoods into the mainstream of American commercial life with concomitant amenities and services that others might take for granted," to say nothing of the "possibility of achieving upward mobility without having to escape to the suburbs or predominantly white neighborhoods."

At the same time, the legacy of racist housing policies, like redlining, and the persistent exploitation of communities of color can inspire a countervailing cynicism. "Many see these improvements as the result of active collaboration between public officials, commercial interests, and white residents," constituting proof that amenities "are only provided when whites move into their neighborhoods."[17] Some may wish to continue to take advantage of repaired roads or better-funded schools as ballooning portions of their income go to rent or property taxes, perhaps deciding that enjoying such amenities amidst the remnants of their community is worth the cost. Others eventually find themselves picking up the pieces of their lives in cheaper municipalities, in the living rooms of friends or family, or under the overpasses of their own city. For them, a place where they were at home is theirs no more. "What it really boils down to," says Daniel González, a father of two from San José, "is that I really don't have that much control over my life and my surroundings and neither do the people who live in the communities that I grew up in."[18]

There are no monuments mourning those forced out, no state assistance programs for the displaced. They are physically removed and then erased from memory, as well. Perhaps a mural or a plaza that the displaced community had created for itself will be left behind, preserved as a macabre trophy for those who pushed them away. It is commonplace for the vanquished to be forgotten or tokenized by their conquerors. As resistance to removal grips cities around the world, there is no room for time-worn theories about liberation that leave as little room for the actual struggles of the gentrified as do the narratives of the powerful.

This book is an attempt to center those engaged in a fight against displacement and for home and land. It suggests that these struggles are not peripheral to the "real" work of workplace organizing, party-building, radical collective formation, or vote-mongering, but the leading edge of confrontation with the contemporary ruling class. It is an effort to re-articulate the relationship between wider resistances and neighborhood defense, to explore the changes in the production and distribution of goods and people that make such struggles necessary, and to provoke new consideration of how we might fight alongside one another for lives dignified and plentiful and free.

***

Gentrification is commonly understood as a pattern of consumption: who chooses to rent or purchase which housing unit. From this perspective we can ask many questions: why white people wish to live in "gritty" neighborhoods, or why they have the opposite attitudes of their parents and grandparents whose white flight bankrupted the cities they abandoned for segregated suburbs. We can debate whether the true villains in the story of neighborhood displacement are the punks and artists, or the yuppies, or the coffee shop patrons, or all white people who move into neighborhoods of color, or any people at all who move into neighborhoods where rents are on the rise. We might wonder at the confluence of factors that make a specific neighborhood appealing for different suspects at different times. And we can play the parlor game of deciding to what degree someone is or is not a gentrifier based on complex tabulations of identities, oppressions, and experiences.

What we cannot do is move beyond the liberal middle-class sport of achieving moral righteousness through carefully curated consumption: the ethical consumerism that pretends to change the world through the thoughtful selection of the correct can from the grocery store shelves. Analyzing gentrification exclusively through the critique of individual consumer preferences ignores the socio-economic and political structures within which these preferences prevail. The scope of the anti-gentrification struggle is reduced to the moral turpitude within a new resident's soul. And all the while, business districts are planned, tax abatements unveiled, redevelopment schemes dreamed up, corporate and university campuses expanded, neighborhoods transformed, and communities destroyed.

Local movements against displacement almost inevitably run up against state power. Far from being an automatic or inevitable process, gentrification is "purposeful and produced."[19] In the mid-twentieth century, the US government began a concerted project of racial displacement from urban areas. The 1938 Federal Housing Administration *Underwriting Manual* recommends a "high speed traffic artery" be placed to protect property values from "adverse influences" such as "lower class occupancy" and "inharmonious racial groups."[20] After World War II, over one million people were displaced to construct an interstate highway system modeled on Germany's Reichsautobahn, with communities of color intentionally targeted.[21] "Our categorical imperative is action to clear the slums," said Robert Moses, the hugely influential urban planner who masterminded public works projects in New York City for decades. Described by a biographer as "the most racist human being I had ever really encountered,"[22] the New York City Planning Commissioner and chair of the Slum Clearance Committee would continue: "We can't let minorities dictate that this century-old chore will be put off another generation or finally abandoned."[23]

Deindustrialization and white flight drained municipal coffers as elites invested in a repressive War on Drugs. Ryan Lugalia-Hollon and Daniel Cooper point out that this might more accurately be described as a War on Neighborhoods, with working-class, Black urban communities framed by politicians as particular dangers to be subdued.[24] After withdrawing services and protection to attack urban neighborhoods of color, cities now court professional workers and their employers to build out their tax bases. The further elimination or privatization of social services goes hand-in-hand with increased investment in policing and infrastructure to smooth the process of displacement and attract capital for "redevelopment." The residents who ultimately benefit from neighborhood change are not the first wave of white punks or artists but the professionals who inhabit the fully gentrified neighborhood.

"When Microsoft, Boeing, and other large corporations started to build in Seattle, they wanted to move their mostly white employees into these areas. They worked with banks and politicians to essentially pressure people into selling," explains Dezmond Goff of Seattle's Black Frontline Movement. "You have a lot of people who lost homes through both predatory loans and harassment but also people who now can't participate because they have been incarcerated."[25]

Intensive investment in redevelopment results from the accelerating allocation of housing resources through market rationality. The US housing market is heavily financialized, driven not by local or regional banks but by huge multinational financial institutions such as private equity firms. During the Savings & Loan Crisis of the 1980s, the federal government acquired properties held by failing banks, grouped them together into huge portfolios, and sold them off together to larger companies. After the 2008 Great Recession, private equity firm Blackstone began purchasing fore-closed single-family homes at discounted rates.[26] As of 2019, it rented out 82,260 houses considered "rent backed structured securities," financial instruments in which investors may purchase bonds.[27] The Great Recession stemmed from escalating defaults on subprime mortgages, the high interest home loans disproportion-ately given to even affluent Black borrowers. In the ensuing crisis, 47.6 percent of Black familial wealth was destroyed as real estate was transferred to firms to Blackstone.[28] The single-family home rental market grew quickly in the wake of this dispossession. In 2021, 24 percent of home sales were to investors, not homeowners, with Black and Hispanic neighborhoods particular targets.[29]

In practice, real estate financialization is the latest face of racial capitalism, the expropriation from (and of) Black and Indigenous peoples, the valuation of labor and life on the basis of race, and the seizure of land based on the same. Predatory lending, state violence, and forced displacement are "inseparable from the violence of the plantation and of settler colonial expansion."[30] For communities of color to be "taken over by wealthier people, pushing out long-time residents" is "essentially the history of the United States," says Liz González, a co-founder of the South Bay Community Land Trust and opponent of the San José Google campus. But modern displacement through the logic of finance capitalism can also be described as a form of neoliberalism, the subordination of increas-ing domains of social life to free-market rationalization and the promotion of the idea that the proper role of the capitalist state is not merely overseeing the market but forcing the expansion of market behavior and opening new resources to investment and exchange. The neoliberal state governs "for the market, rather than because of the market," actively intervening so that the conditions for new fields of capitalist behavior might be "carefully and artificially constructed."[31] Freed from the sentimentality of the small proprietor and the antiquated notion of social housing as a public good, a house is increasingly treated as an asset far more than it is as a home.

From 2015 to 2019, the construction of new housing units in San Francisco was outpaced by the growth in vacancies until 10 percent of the total housing stock sat empty: almost five empty homes for each unhoused person.[32] Two years after the Four Seasons high rise condo development opened, 133 of its 146 units remained empty—including San Francisco's most expensive penthouse, listed at $49 million.[33] Half of Manhattan's new luxury condominiums were vacant in 2019.[34] But the failure of a unit to find a resident does not mean it has not appreciated in value for its owner. The growing amount of capital invested in real estate-as-asset has caused the valuation of housing to reach "historically unprecedented heights, implying that real estate has become more important as store-of-value in the age of financialization." The centrality of housing and land in the generation, storage, and transfer of wealth is so pronounced that some speak of contemporary capitalism as a "real estate-driven regime of accumulation."[35]

By itself, the fact that financial institutions have become the predominant players in the neoliberal housing market isn't enough to explain why gentrification takes place in modern cities. In the settler colonial imperial heartland, the construction, movement, and survival of oppressed communities has always been contingent on their utility to capitalist interests. The communities displaced today have been subjected to double or triple displacements long before: from the horrors of the Middle Passage to the killing fields of the US-sponsored Dirty Wars to the fatal nighttime cold of the Sonoran Desert. The history of the United States could be written as the story of colonial dispossession and relocation for profit, but what is emerging today is a new pattern of urban dispersal. Hedge funds or institutional landlords concerned only with their own wealth could choose to invest in vast slums or modest homes for the lower-middle class. In the gentrifying city, what they find most profitable is to bet on slum clearance and invest in condominiums for the rich. The patterns of impoverishment and displacement are old, the directionality of urban displacement is new. "So to answer the question of why gentrification happens," writes P. E. Moskowitz, "we have to answer the question of why the city became profitable to gentrify."[36]

For comparison, I might harbor a deep-seated desire to own a Beverly Hills mansion. Books could be written about how I acquired such an inclination, about the social structures that induce such desires, or about what this preference says about me or the society in which I live. They would remain hypothetical texts since my desire to live in such a mansion would not change my inability to purchase one. It is a consumption preference I will never fulfill.

Only the complete transformation of a poor neighborhood creates the living standards, amenities, and neighbors that professional-class newcomers desire. Unlike my hypothetical mansion aspirations, these are desires they do fulfill, not only one-by-one but in cities across the world. Regardless of any person's desire to live in an expensive condominium at a certain address, there is the matter of being paid enough to afford it. What has shifted over the years is not simply the living preferences of white Americans but the relative economic centrality of two class fractions: one segment paid enough to gentrify, another paid so little that they are priced out. A highly educated, largely white segment of working people are now paid astronomical wages while the remains of the urban industrial working class, previously crucial to capitalist profits, are now of so little importance that the utter destruction of their communities is a lucrative venture. To understand this process in rich nations' richest cities, to situate it within the context of a broad economic transition in global capitalism, and to grasp how thoroughly this change must unsettle our inherited strategies of how to uproot this world, we must look at gentrification not only from the perspective of consumption but production, as well. The struggles around urban displacement are some of the clearest fractures emerging from what has been called the New Economy, the Knowledge Economy, or the Fourth Industrial Revolution, an economic arrangement within contemporary capitalism that we might as easily name the Gentrification Economy.[37]

***

Though we will begin in Silicon Valley, this urban reconfiguration is by no means a story of regional interest. Cities as diverse as Bangalore, Cairo, Lima, Rio de Janeiro, and Shanghai are all undergoing "urban bourgeiosification." Even growing metropolitan areas are simultaneously expelling working-class residents from neighborhoods desirable to domestic professionals or international tourists.[38]

The first section of this book will explore the city as a site of resistance and contestation, a space whose changing contours form the content of struggles against displacement and the context for many other struggles besides. The following chapter will examine the inhabitance of place, the violence of dislocation, and the forms of knowledge and relations proper to residence and replacement. We will investigate the connection between transplanted workers and a transformation of work, seeing how new configurations of exploitation and labor structure the gentrifying city and the struggles within and beyond it. After looking at gentrification as a conscious project by state and corporate elites that requires co-optation and pacification as well as repression and terror, we close with a provisional investigation into emergent possibilities suggested by contemporary struggles against displacement and racial capitalism, the motor of the gentrification economy.

Sporadic language throughout is borrowed from an article previously published by *Notes From Below*, written after several years' participation in anti-displacement struggles in California's Silicon Valley.[39] This book is limited by the perspective of its author, college-educated, raised in a non-gentrifying neighborhood in the United States, and possessing the resources to compose it, if also someone who washed dishes dirtied by the "cognitive elite" while living out of a portion of a converted garage. This book attempts to overcome these constraints in part by centering and building off of the experiences, analyses, and strategies of a diverse, though necessarily partial, set of those fighting displacement in different areas.

It is in no way a set of guidelines for those in struggle or benchmarks by which struggle may be judged by those on the sidelines. Around the world, collectives and organizations, collaborators and friends are advancing the struggle against forced displacement in myriad directions, shutting down developments and evictions and bringing cities to a halt, struggling against militarized police and the most powerful companies in the world. Those in struggle chart the way forward.

I. SPACE

"All space is occupied by the enemy. We are living under a permanent curfew. Not just the cops—the geometry."
—*Raoul Vaneigem*

In the United States, gentrification is most associated with the cities of the San Francisco Bay Area: San Francisco, Oakland, and San José and the rest of Silicon Valley to the south. As Ground Zero for the consumer tech industry, a major driver of the gentrification economy, this region presents perhaps the most advanced domestic example of the process to date.

Firms like Hewlett-Packard were cornerstones of the military-industrial complex before pivoting to consumer sales with the wind-down of the Cold War. Home to both a major military installation in Oakland and a stream of educated prospective employees and investment capital from Stanford University, the Bay Area proved an ideal location for the modern tech industry to develop.

Today, the area is home to a bevy of the richest companies in the world, from Google and Facebook to Chevron, Wells Fargo, and Lockheed Martin. A network of venture capitalists, coding boot camps, and office parks feed the key industries of finance, tech, and biotech. Glossy condos and trendy restaurants serve their workers.

It is a region of mind-boggling wealth. The greater Silicon Valley now has an annual GDP rivaling that of Saudi Arabia.

The allure of rich cities and boomtowns for fortune-seeking newcomers is nothing new. Those living in the countryside, in outlying towns, and in less-affluent areas, sometimes a country or ocean away, have long uprooted their lives for a chance at wealth or simply survival. It is not at all surprising that people are likewise drawn to the San Francisco Bay Area of today, from bright-eyed computer science graduates looking for a six-figure job on a tech campus to those hoping to clean its toilets or work its dish room. The populations of wealthy areas swell as newcomers arrive hoping to strike gold.

The curious thing is the degree to which this is not occurring in the contemporary Bay Area. One of the wealthiest areas in the world is shedding low-wage workers. From 2010 to 2016, 1.5 million people moved out—roughly one in five residents. Their numbers were masked by a continual flow of new arrivals whose incomes skewed appreciably higher than those they replaced.[1] San José, "Capital of Silicon Valley," saw negative population growth in 2019, a year before the COVID-19 pandemic reached the US.[2] It is a pattern shared with many of the wealthiest cities in East Asia, Europe, and North America, even as the continued growth of poorer cities ensures that the urban share of the global population continues to rise.[3]

As late as the 1990s, one in every five workers in San José still worked in low-wage electronics assembly, the industry that prompted the area's urbanization.[4] The concentration of exploited workers right next to the wealth of tech magnates spurred formal and informal organizing efforts. In the 1980s, the United Electrical, Radio and Machine Workers of America organizing committee of Silicon Valley factory workers numbered five hundred. When a committee leader at a Versatronex plant was fired, workers brought up in the Mexican student and labor movements launched an occupation and hunger strike.[5]

It was a time when the words of Engels and Marx still rang true:

> The bourgeoisie keeps more and more doing away with the scattered state of the population, of the means of production, and of property. It has agglomerated population, centralized the means of production, and has concentrated property in a few hands. . . . But with the development of industry the proletariat not only increases in number; it becomes concentrated in greater masses, its strength grows, and it feels its strength more. . . . Thereupon, the workers begin to form combinations [labor unions] against the bourgeois; they club together in order to keep up wages. They enter into long-term associations in order to make provision beforehand for these occasional revolts. Here and there the struggle breaks out into riots.[6]

Whether in the auto plants of Detroit, the electronics assembly lines of San José, or the Manchester textile factories described in the *Manifesto*, urbanization and the industrial centralization of workers multiplied the leverage that could be applied at the point of production against a shared employer. In that world, there was a figure increasingly concentrated spatially, in the world's wealthiest cities, and economically, working for the same growing companies. Her impoverishment gave her reason to revolt, her convergence with others of the same condition gave her the means to do so, and her strategic position in key industries in the centers of the global economy meant that her revolt would shake the halls of power. These three factors gave rise to the theory that this figure was the one who could therefore truly transform the world by virtue of being a member of a class named proletariat.[7]

And in 1871, the members of this class held Paris for two months, declaring the Commune in the city Walter Benjamin named the nineteenth century's "capital." A century later, the Situationist International would call the Paris Commune "the only implementation of a revolutionary urbanism to date."[8] The struggle of the urban proletariat forged the tactical toolbox of all branches of the Left: the commune, the union, the general strike, electoral socialism. The revolutionary party, the affinity group, the workers' militia, and direct action were born of this struggle, as well. Today, we are told that the capital of the twenty-first century is the Bay Area, the very same region that is rapidly expelling hundreds of thousands of low-wage workers out of brute economic interest. The world's capital has moved. We are no longer needed in it.

manufacturing. For the most part, the great assembly lines that drew in workers for tedious, monotonous, but reasonably compensated jobs are gone. Electronics manufacture has almost entirely left Silicon Valley. Neither Apple, Broadcom, nor Nvidia own the semiconductor foundries that produce the chips they design. Instead, they depend on an array of subcontractors who largely manufacture in South Korea, Taiwan, Japan, and, increasingly, China, where the development of "new-type industrialization" and "a new pattern of opening up" are emphasized as long-term goals in the fourteenth Five-Year Plan.[13]

The wake created by the departure of electronics assembly from Silicon Valley was largely filled by service and maintenance jobs. Outsourcing and automation have made a working population once critical to investors now in many ways inconsequential to their quarterly profits. In San José, one of the richest cities in the United States, the "capital" of a region whose name is popularly associated with opportunity and young wealth, the average service industry worker's salary of $35,241 is shockingly close to the $25,800 it costs to rent the average studio apartment.[14] This leaves $26 a day for all the remaining necessities of life, an absurdity in one of the most expensive markets in the US. Renting space in living rooms and garages is commonplace. In 2019, a San Francisco closet went for $1,200 a month.[15] A woman living in a three-bedroom house with a dozen occupants in San Mateo got COVID-19 and was forced to decamp to a closet: it was the only free space in her home where she could be sure not to pass the virus to her children.[16]

"I pay $475 for half of a room in a house that has no air conditioning, no heating, no laundry. Our shower is a converted closet. We've had rats. We've had cockroaches. Our window screen is a bunch of chicken wire nailed to a two by four. And that's a good deal," says Emerald, a housing activist on the board of directors of the South Bay Community Land Trust.[17] The faculty at Cupertino's

De Anza College, one of the top-rated community colleges in the nation, voted to allow the 20 percent of students who are homeless to sleep overnight in their cars in the campus parking lot.[18] This suffering is obscured from newly arriving professionals since the dynamics of displacement are not uniformly distributed across the metropolis. Many engineers on the Google campus in Mountain View remained blissfully unaware that a park two miles away was almost completely encircled by RVs serving as the new homes of the evicted.[19]

"In our area, if you're making $117,000, you're considered low-income. People who aren't making $117,000 can't afford affordable housing here. People are extremely rent-burdened, doubling up into apartments, multiple families in single-family homes, and apartments in conditions that are really unlivable, paying exorbitant rent. This is normal here," says Liz González.[20]

Silicon and Rust

"People always have a natural aversion to innovation."
—*Alphabet CEO Sergey Brin*

The cities of the Rust Belt, with their plummeting populations and depleted city coffers, are sometimes held up as negative examples against the success stories of cities like San Francisco and Austin. "How can we, as a nation, maximize the chances that our innovation hubs follow the path of the San Francisco-Silicon Valley cluster and not that of Detroit and Rochester?" writes economist Enrico Moretti.[21] As the example of Silicon Valley shows, the obliteration and dispersal of an industrial base and the impoverishment of those Moretti calls "low-skilled workers" is necessary for "high-skilled workers" to be able to descend upon these so-called "innovation hubs." Dispossession and deprivation in the wake of outsourcing and automation is as necessary for the modern Bay Area as it is for contemporary Detroit, a "global metaphor for capitalist decline" after waves of deindustrialization from the 1950s to 1970s.[22] In 1958, Detroit's 3.5 million square foot Packard Automotive Plant was abandoned after Studebaker-Packard moved production to South Bend, Indiana—only to end US automobile production entirely three years later.[23] Though the Packard building in Detroit remains empty, Ford purchased Michigan Central Station, mothballed in 2018, to make a "new mobility innovation district" for "mobility innovators and disruptors from around the world."[24]

Large cities on the hunt for economic growth aspire to more than the arrival of one new employer or mixed-use building. The industrializing city had certain requirements: railroads to ship commodities, slums to house workers, machines to fill the sweatshops, and the laborers to work them. The modern "innovation hub" also has preconditions, among them an ecosystem of amenities to attract well-paid technical employees. This means green-lighting new housing and office developments, supporting the creation of retail districts where new residents might dine and shop, and municipal investments in policing and infrastructure to create a habitat appealing to corporate employees and conducive to business operations. Such massive, interconnected projects are most profitable when constructed on top of districts with diminished land values that are close to infrastructure and potential commercial corridors.

Attempts to create such an ecosystem in one fell swoop include massive redevelopment projects such as the plans by Google/Alphabet subsidiary Sidewalk Labs to create a "smart city" along Toronto's waterfront. The proposal for the "IDEA district" ballooned from twenty to 190 acres, with development to begin in the Quayside neighborhood, an "underutilized," "post-industrial piece of land" situated close to downtown "at the nexus of many key corridors."[25] The company's comprehensive plan for the eastern waterfront included housing, offices, shops, and "civic amenities," with infrastructure investment to "unlock" new neighborhoods. Google's Canadian HQ would relocate there to form the keystone of an "innovation campus."[26] The city of Toronto would see its property tax revenue triple as "complete communities" attracted new employees.[27] The "active collaboration between public officials, commercial interests, and white residents" cited in the introduction is evident.[28]

The IDEA district soon became a lightning rod for controversy. Google hoped to achieve massive data collection through sensors embedded throughout the development to create what Sidewalk Labs CEO Dan Doctoroff had called a "Google City" whose "urban data" would comprise a "test bed and product/service trial venue."[29] An organization called Block Sidewalk coalesced against "ubiquitous surveillance," the massive transfer of municipal property (in actuality the occupied territory of the Mississaugas of the Credit First Nation) to American developers and tech firms, and fears of Silicon Valley-type gentrification.[30] Though the company conveniently attributed the project's cancellation in May 2020 to COVID-19-related "economic uncertainty,"[31] Block Sidewalk's organizers recognized it as the result of community mobilization. "This is huge, we are sending a message to Silicon Valley on behalf of all those around the world who are fighting big tech in their cities. The Quayside project got mangled down from an 800-acres vision of a surveillance state to a bid for an office building on a 12-acre site. We knew all along that Sidewalk can't realize its tech dreams on 12-acres alone, so this has been coming for a while," said Block Sidewalk's Julie Beddoes. As Thorden Wieditz added, "This outcome is a testament to the principled and courageous stance taken by citizens to protect Toronto from Google's corporate takeover. Without the on-the-ground organizing and the commitment of so many individuals, groups and organizations, this would have not been possible."[32]

what the company in whose buildings we worked actually produced. It was irrelevant: campus food, custodial, and security services are subcontracted, so workers were always moving to other campuses, either one by one or en masse if their employer lost the contract. Our supervisor told us to "be seen but not heard" when we brought hot lunches for executive meetings or bussed tables at conferences. The company's full-time employees seemed to not see us even as we lugged heavy chafing dishes behind them in narrow conference rooms. To understand the condition of being present but absent, you must distinguish between "membership and inclusion, between what is outside and inside."[36] It should be no surprise that luxuries for the affluent are undergirded not only by exploitation but also by the arbitrary violence of white supremacist policing, ICE raids, and terminations without cause.

Students and workers on university and corporate campuses are encouraged to look inwards, away from the larger city and those who serve them: the very objective of the campus as institution. The longstanding, particularly American tradition of building residence halls for university students is designed to enforce the separation of students—traditionally white, male, upper-class—from the temptations of the city beyond, supporting moral edification through the construction of fraternity exclusively between those within.[37] While a professor at Princeton University, Woodrow Wilson emphasized the importance of the detached university campus for the inculcation of "liberal culture" among an elite distinguished from "the majority who carry forward the common labor of the world."[38] The university campus is the model for the urban corporate campus, which similarly shields members from the world beyond. Silicon Valley tech campuses provide employees with free gyms, cafeterias, and recreational facilities. Private buses shuttle techies from their homes to the office without subjecting them to the indignities of public transportation. One of Facebook's Menlo Park office buildings is capped with a private nine-acre rooftop park, with a half-mile walking trail winding between hundreds of trees.[39] As with the elite college student, those working in such "exclusive utopias with limited interactions with their surroundings" inhabit a world where displacement might appear a far-off abstraction.[40] The lives of those cleaning the bathrooms of those very same campuses must seem to them a world away entirely.

In the gentrifying city, the most attractive service jobs are within and around the campuses, office parks, and commercial districts where the cost of living is most prohibitive. Alongside grandiose keystone projects there exists a more piecemeal process of transformation that is at first "tightly concentrated in specific blocks and neighborhoods"[41] from which new residents spread out one-by-one. Some are wealthy, professional-class new arrivals, others are themselves displaced from already gentrifying neighborhoods. More often than not, this process has an explicitly racial character.

In 1979, geographer Neil Smith argued that currently undervalued urban neighborhoods are those most susceptible to gentrification, since the gap between the present and potential future value of a piece of property represents the profits available to capitalists who invest in "revitalization."[42] One of the largest determinants of neighborhood devaluation is the race of its residents. Houses in majority-Black neighborhoods are valued half as highly as those in neighborhoods with no Black residents, with houses occupied by their Black owners undervalued by an average of $48,000. The value of a property can appreciate by tens of thousands of extra dollars should the racial composition of its neighborhood change through mass displacement.[43]

"Neighborhoods that don't have great amenities, like community centers, grocery stores, or other things people need to survive day-to-day, present an opportunity to increase the profit margin by such a huge gap because these neighborhoods, not too long ago, didn't see public housing or any type of investment," says Vasudha, a Silicon Valley activist and scholar.[44] "A lot of real estate and redevelopment projects will focus on disinvested neighborhoods because the profit margin there will be sky-high, and they can make so much money off of just a little bit of investment in that area."

The residents of the neighborhoods most liable to gentrification are therefore often Black or brown, and the gentrifiers who push them out are typically the white (or sometimes East and South Asian) workers who monopolize lucrative professional jobs at many firms. In 2020, Google's workforce was just 5.9 percent Latinx and only 3.7 percent Black.[45] These largely white, well-off workers may find moving into a majority-Black or brown neighborhood more palatable should a number of white artists, students, or punks make the move first. Social and spatial racial segregation, white supremacy, and white solidarity are so powerful that the most uptight software engineer might imagine relatively friendly faces in the crustiest of punk houses.[46]

"What's infuriating is that, the history of Boyle Heights is that a lot of us were forced to live here," says Los Angeles playwright Josefina Lopez. "It was the ghetto, right. [That] was the way it was viewed. And once we've made it beautiful, people go, 'Oh yeah, let me take it from you now.'"[47]

The net result is that within the gentrifying city, low-wage workers, especially workers of color, remain economically tied to the affluent city core while accessible housing options move farther and farther away. These cities may see their wealth rise, even as their populations drop, unlike the growing metropoles of the Industrial Revolution. And unlike in non-gentrifying post-industrial cities, it is wealth and not poverty that is concentrated.

Urbanist Alan Ehrenhalt describes the "Great Inversion," the contemporary "reversal in which the words 'inner city,' which a generation ago connoted poverty and slums, [are going to mean] the home of wealthier people who have a choice about where they live, and the suburbs are going to be the home of immigrants and poorer people."[48] Cities around the United States are realigning to the pattern of nineteenth-century Vienna or present-day Mexico City and Paris: "an affluent and stylish urban core surrounded by poorer people and an immigrant working class on the periphery."[49]

Concentrations of industrial workers still exist in the United States: "giant food processing plants in exurban areas; energy extraction centers on Appalachian mountaintops and Gulf coast outposts; and, most importantly for big cities, growing import/ export processing zones in major metropolitan areas."[50] However, they are largely absent from urban areas proper. After World War II, corporations intentionally shifted production from Northeastern cities to the "weakly organized regions of the Sunbelt or the Midwestern rural periphery" to break the power of organized labor, inaugurating a new, decentralized "union-resistant geography" of industrial production in the United States.[51]

Outside the US, cities are still built around the proletarian drudgery of manufacturing in large factories: Ciudad Juárez in Mexico, Shenzhen in mainland China.[52] And within post-industrial gentrifying cities, workers still sell their labor for poverty wages, if not joining the unemployed labor reserve waiting to take the place of currently employed workers. In fact, it is the deprivation of working-class residents that expose their neighborhoods to gentrification. It remains the case that the gentrifying city presents a radically distinct terrain of exploitation and resistance in an era when cities assume an even greater role in the capitalist system.

The Weight of the Dead

"The city has been the historical battleground of the struggle for freedom, but it has yet to host its victory."

—*Guy Debord*

The elections of Bolsonaro, Johnson, and Trump in the late 2010s heralded the vengeful reappearance of nationalism as legitimating ideology in Western countries. Their explicit appeals to national interests marked not the resurgent strength of the nation-state but rather its historic weakness.[53] And it is just at the moment that the class dynamics of wealthy municipalities transformed that cities have gained increasing importance within the global system.

"I think we have to understand that the nation-state became powerful in the wake of the French Revolution, whereas the nation-state has become powerless in light of globalization," noted Grace Lee Boggs in 2014.[54] While the subsumption of national autonomy within global Empire has been exaggerated, national governments have quietly ceded domains of activity to both transnational institutions and the sub-national governments within them. Large metropolitan "city-regions" are emerging from the nations that house them to "take on definite identity and force as economic and political actors on the world stage."[55] Interconnected labor and capital flows that join national economies, intergovernmental organizations and multinational agreements, and the neoliberal privatization of state functions all comprise relative constraints on nation-state autonomy.[56] Urban populations are redistributed as major cities find themselves competing against each other "in the global market, shorn of much of the traditional protection of national state institutions and regulations. . . . In this context, gentrification became a hallmark of the emerging 'global city.'"[57]

The city has acquired increased importance in defining the conditions for global capital accumulation, but it has always played an outsized, if under-appreciated, role in the politics of the left. The entire left-right distinction in politics descends from the French Revolution, initiated by riots in the streets of Paris, but much revolutionary left strategy seeks to answer the question posed by the Paris Commune: how might oppressed peoples establish political hegemony over urban space? The city was the only thinkable terrain for the revolutionary urban Commune, the *soviets* of the Russian Revolution, the anarchist administration of Barcelona, the Black Panther Party's ascendance in Oakland, or the early-twenty-first century's Movement of the Squares, including Occupy Wall Street in the United States.

Against urbanist leftism, a competing thread of thought and practice instead views rural areas as the ideal terrain for class struggle. But even insurgencies that played out in the countryside often first appeared in protean form in cities, which provided a staging ground for the accumulation of forces. Non-Mayan elements of the Ejercito Zapatista de Liberación Nacional descended from the Fuerzas de Liberación Nacional, an organization based not in rural Chiapas but in Mexico's second-largest city of Monterrey.[58] The famed anarchist peasant collectives of revolutionary Spain were in fact sometimes "installed forcibly" by anarchist industrial workers "[impatient] to get the harvest in to feed the cities" such as Barcelona, where the Confederación Nacional de Trabajo had four hundred thousand members.[59]

Ex-anarchist Mao Zedong introduced "a powerful anti-urban bias foreign to the Marxist tradition" with his formulation of

Protracted People's War.[60] It is far from clear that this strategy would have achieved predominance had the repression of urban labor militancy not first displaced Communist Party cadre from movement strongholds like Shanghai and Canton.[61] And the Cuban Revolution, which birthed the *foco* theory of rural guerrilla warfare, was preceded by urban rebellions of radical student groups and labor unions in the early 1950s. It was the pressure of urban organizations like the Federación Estudiantil Universitaria that secured Fidel Castro's release from prison, allowing him to initiate his eventually successful guerrilla campaign in the first place.

The above historical examples arrive from disparate cultural, political, and economic contexts.[62] The common ground underlying each was the spatial concentration of impoverished workers in a city they tried to claim as their own, a common ground eroded day-by-day in a gentrifying city from which the oppressed are instead pushed away. The radically different material conditions of the key cities and financial hubs of contemporary advanced capitalist nations do not prevent popular struggle. Indeed, those in struggle today, including those not explicitly organizing against urban displacement, are already grappling with this new terrain in practice, in the streets.

Defending Urban Space

"Revolution is based on land. Land is the basis for all independence. Land is the basis of freedom, justice, and equality."

—*Malcolm X*

Reacting to a financial crisis that led to the eviction of millions, Occupy Wall Street was an effort to congeal a revolutionary force while formulating a radical, prefigurative demonstration of non-capitalist social relations. It is significant that the staging grounds for this project were largely central plazas and squares in urban areas. While banks and sheriffs worked to effect the mass displacement and dispersal of homeowners and tenants, Occupy responded with audacious claims of a popular right to the city.

There are ongoing efforts to enforce this right through community land trusts (CLTs), which acquire land and lease the buildings on top of it to residents, businesses, or cooperatives. But the trust holds the land underneath these buildings in perpetuity, insulating it from the inflating prices of overheated housing markets. Since this land is held in trust permanently, it is effectively removed from the speculative market: the immediate decommodification of land. One challenge of this model is the piecemeal acquisition of property. For properties to be acquired through the market, the CLT must provide exorbitant amounts of money, especially in the gentrifying cities where this intervention is most needed. Sometimes allies can be persuaded to donate properties to the trust. In other instances, CLTs and affiliated organizations launch political campaigns against landowners, usually public agencies, to "donate" the land themselves. For months, unhoused people held two Occupy-style protest encampments in Philadelphia while mothers and children occupied fifteen vacant city-owned homes, eventually pressuring the Philadelphia Housing Authority to agree to donate fifty homes to a CLT.[63]

Liberated spaces and squats also represent defensive maneuvers to maintain urban space in the face of displacement. West Oakland's Qilombo and the adjacent Afrikatown garden replaced a predominantly white anarchist space in the wake of a community accountability process.[64] Qilombo served as a horizontally organized Afrikan and Indigenous community center for over four years before being evicted in 2019.[65] Encampments and liberated spaces can also serve as the stage for a pivot towards offensive tactics. Occupy birthed a host of political collectives and housing justice campaigns that continued even after police cleared the encampments. Qilombo was built as "a center for Afrikan resistance" aimed at "[fostering] a network of black and brown folks dedicated to dismantling capitalism and anti-blackness."[66] In 2013, the school district in Seattle's historically Black, gentrifying Central District (CD) issued an illegal eviction notice for organizations operating community services out of space rented in a former school. Resisters were eventually forced out at gunpoint.[67]

"We see the use of police violence to stop people from making community," says Dezmond Goff of Seattle's Black Frontline Movement. "If people were able to establish this community center, this cultural space for Black people in the CD, it could be the beginning of an entire cultural resurgence and resistance to gentrification at large."[68]

Sandy Perry of the South Bay Community Land Trust and Affordable Housing Network likewise envisions a community center on decommodified land serving as an organizing space to launch initiatives against further dispossession, a base area that would "give a whole community a center around which to organize."[69] To hold and defend contested space necessarily implies not only a revolutionary posture but also the creation of different ways of being and being-together.

Disrupting Circulation

"Let us devastate the avenues where the wealthy live."
—*Lucy Parsons*

Within the city, affluent young professionals often prefer biking or public transportation to car ownership. "Mixed-use projects" that incorporate housing, food, and retail options aimed at gentrifiers often spring up in "transit-oriented developments" around public transportation hubs.

"Having easy access to public transportation should not become a luxury that is extended only to the affluent," says Justine Bayod Espoz of Chicago's Somos Logan Square, an organization that led a lockdown blockade of a transit-oriented development construction site in 2016.[70] Transit-oriented developments are advertised as victories for sustainability and environmentalism, the result of "politically neutral planning that is consensual as well as ecologically and socially sensitive." The creation of such projects in practice "subordinates equity to profit-minded development" to the extent that their supposed ecological benefits evaporate.[71] Insofar as displaced residents are forced to commute longer distances to work after being displaced by eco-friendly, transit-oriented development projects, these projects can actually increase metropolitan carbon emissions.[72]

The dislocation of poor workers from the urban core forces many to commute from homes in cheaper suburbs back to jobs in expensive cities in which they once lived themselves.[73] In the San Francisco Bay Area, low-wage workers are increasingly moving to the cities of the Central Valley and other outlying areas. In 2017, 170,000 people commuted from neighboring counties to work jobs in the Bay Area; eighty-six thousand commuted at least sixty miles.[74]

"A lot of people have moved there from LA because the cost of housing was just way too high. When I go now, it's unrecognizable," says Jenna of Southern California's High Desert. "They have all this commercial development, but there's still no jobs. Most people that live there have to commute hours to get to work anywhere."[75] Both professional-oriented transit development and the lengthening commutes of low-paid displaced workers increase the importance of transportation networks to the metropolitan economy.

The youth-led, anti-capitalist "spontaneous popular uprising" of the Estallito Social spread across Chile after high school students responded to a dramatic metro fare hike by jumping the metro turnstiles in Santiago.[76] In the city of six million, "Anglo-style gentrification," intensive capital reinvestment displacing the poor from the city center, is joined by a housing subsidy program that "expels the most vulnerable, in exchange for a roof, farther and farther out into the city's periphery."[77] Whereas American urban areas concentrated poverty after deindustrialization, Santiago follows the pattern of many Latin American cities where the very poor live in largely informal, unregulated settlements at the city's edge. But the urban periphery is now also targeted by developers buying up cheap land for planned suburban housing developments marketed to the middle class. "Over the next generation," it is projected that "suburban expansion will only continue this phenomenon, driving low-income *Santiaguinos* further out, placing greater strains on public transit and increasing their already long commute times."[78]

The original direct actions against fare increases took place in the strategic context of ever-more "intense circulation of commodities, people, and capital between the city center and its hinterland," thanks to such expansion.[79]

When the 2014 police murder of Michael Brown sparked an uprising, residents of the suburban town of Ferguson, Missouri, repeatedly gathered on West Florissant, a four-lane highway leading into St. Louis.[80] Subsequent Black Lives Matter demonstrations frequently targeted highways as strategic chokepoints. In May 2020, an autonomous, leaderless demonstration in San José held down the 101—the highway connecting San José and San Francisco—for almost an hour.[81] Across the country, radicals found that the vital weakness of the city was the transportation infrastructure necessary for the circulation of workers in, out, and through the metropolis.

"The way cities are organized in Orange County really requires you to have a car. Santa Ana is pretty much the only city that has good public transit, and it's really hard to take a bus between cities. The freeways were the most impactful way to disrupt business as usual: putting your body on the line to stop the everyday commute. Because it's met with so much police resistance, it feels like you're touching on something and actually creating a disturbance, whereas sometimes when you're shouting at City Hall, it feels like you're yelling into the void," says Jenna.[82] From this perspective, liberal-reformist and party-led efforts to divert energy from major freeways into stage-managed marches and rallies not only represented the abandonment of a revolutionary project but also the surrender of the strategic high ground, both metaphorically and literally. As the Círculo de Comunistas Esotéricos wrote of the Chilean uprising, "By turning itself into a citizen's movement [i.e., one negotiating the terms of the social pact between the state and its subjects], the popular spontaneous movement reconfigures the conditions by which it grew and limits its own possibilities of action. It is self-negation and creeping self-sabotage through resorting to the traditional or classic forms of the popular movements of the twentieth century."[83] These forms were elaborated in conditions that no longer prevail in the metropolises of affluent and semi-peripheral countries. "To forget the dead," they continue, "we must first kill them." Only death provides space for the living.

This is not to say that these struggles were "about" gentrification in ways unbeknownst to their participants. Those who risked incarceration or death to weaken the hold of white supremacy or the capitalist state knew quite well what they were doing and why. But every movement, protest, or uprising takes place in a certain space. It may be a city square, a meeting hall, or certain rooms within certain neighborhoods in front of certain laptops or smartphones. Spatial considerations are the price of human embodiment. We are interested here not in making a specious claim about false consciousness. Rather, we are suggesting a line of examination concerning the ways in which the newly changed population distributions of gentrifying cities condition emergent tactical openings for the movements who use them as their theaters. No matter the cause of the revolt, transportation networks in gentrifying cities have proven a critical point of leverage.

But there are things that a map cannot capture, among them the most tragic effects of displacement. People are ripped not just from buildings but from homes. If we consider the essence of a neighborhood not the pavement and street signs but the web of human interrelationships they support, gentrifying neighborhoods are not changed but in fact dismantled and then replaced. As the space of the city is transformed, the places within it are uprooted as well. Grappling with this dynamic will allow us to highlight important features of the process of displacement and the struggle for land.

II. PLACE

"Esta es una comunicación que se da en un territorio específico, en una ciudad limitada. Quizá alguien encuentre aquí elementos en común para poder entender su propio devenir, en otras ciudades, en otros países, en otros continentes."
[This is a communication from a specific territory, in a constrained city. Perhaps someone will be able to find here common elements to understand their own future in other cities, in other countries, on other continents.]

—*Círculo de Comunistas Esotéricos*

Displacement (Spanish: *desplazamiento*) is removal from the plaza, the place. Both plaza and place come from the Greek word *plateia*, the broad road in which the annual processions of Zeus Alseios and Zeus Polieus displayed the social order of the city in objective form. All of which is to say: a place is where things make sense.

A place is where things make sense to us, and where we make sense to others. A place, says Yi-Fu Tuan, is "an object in which one can dwell."[1] Maps portray space, the area in which we move, the roads and buildings between certain coordinates. Place is different.

A place holds value and significance for those who recognize it. Places hold memories, secret knowledges, lingering smells, and restless ghosts. The house where your aunt lived before she died, the park where you had your first kiss, the street whose *real* name is different than the one on the street signs. The unmarked landmarks. The memories we have collectively adhered to the earth.

Gentrification's transformation of *space* as buildings are replaced, infrastructure is improved, and communities are relocated is accompanied by the removal of *places* as those for whom they held meaning are priced out. Given that poor neighborhoods of color are those targeted for expulsion, many of these places are cultural landmarks testifying to community struggle and resistance. And during a process that can seem both unstoppable and abstract, they can become focal points for collective resistance in the present day.

Under the Condos, the Beach

"By a kind of perverted logic, colonialism turns to the past of the oppressed people and distorts, disfigures, and destroys it."

—*Frantz Fanon*

"When we think about the loss of our legacy, we think about the loss of our history, we think of what it is we don't see anymore," says Naomi Nightingale of Los Angeles's Venice neighborhood. "And if you don't see it anymore, you soon forget that it was even there. You pass by certain places and you see an empty space and you say, 'What used to be there?'"[2]

In the early-twentieth century, magnate Abbott Kinney hired Black workers from the South to dig the canals of the "Venice of America" on the Pacific coast. White-only housing codes and the thousands-strong Los Angeles chapter of the KKK limited Black families to one square mile within Venice's Oakwood neighborhood. Oakwood's Black population tripled to fill jobs at the nearby Douglas Aircraft Company factory during World War II, while Latinx families arrived in the 1960s after being displaced with the construction of the Santa Monica Freeway.[3]

"Jobs were plentiful" until the Douglas Aircraft factory closed in 1975, says Venice community leader Jataun Valentine.[4] By the early 1990s, one journalist described Oakwood as "a war zone," a "drug-infested warren of gentrified bungalows and federally subsidized apartment complexes."[5] Though gang violence fell, increased interest in Venice as a "hip" neighborhood incentivized ongoing police attention. A sweeping gang injunction in 2000 facilitated the police harassment of Black Oakwood residents to the degree that a post-funeral ceremony in Oakwood Park was confronted by police in riot gear.[6]

Two years after the injunction was instated, actress Julia Roberts bought a $1.3 million property just south of Oakwood. Today, celebrities, "tech bros," and white-collar film industry professionals live in angular glass and wood houses whose hulking security fences shield them from working-class Black and Latinx families in apartment buildings next door.[7]

In 2017, the pastor of the First Baptist Church of Venice got $6.3 million by selling the church building out from under his congregation to Jay Penske. Penske, owner of a media empire that includes *Variety* and *Rolling Stone,* planned to remodel the interior, install a rooftop deck, and occupy it as a single-family home. Opposition to the sale and remodeling of the church became a lightning rod for community resistance to the conversion of Venice into "an elite enclave for millionaires and tech companies."[8]

Founded in 1910, First Baptist served as a central community institution for generations of Oakwood residents. "When it was to the point where Blacks had to live in a certain area, the church was like that home for them," says Jataun Valentine, whose great uncle was a "pioneer" of the church. Valentine knows three or four families from each street in Oakwood who have already been priced out. Though residents see the changes around them, she says, they don't want to believe what's happening until it happens to them. But the proposed conversion of First Baptist into a white millionaire's private residence galvanized years of protests and vigils and became the central issue of Save Venice, a local anti-displacement group.

"They want to leave the outside like the church but inside it would be their home. That would be like a Hollywood prop," explains Valentine. "Black history in Venice needs to really be known. And First Baptist Church is it."[9] In September 2021, the Save Venice campaign secured the designation of First Baptist as a historical-cultural monument, effectively blocking Penske's renovation.[10] "There is still a road ahead to reclaim [the building] from gentrifiers and restore it back into the community's hands," say Save Venice organizers, and "to finish the rest of the mission to restore and amplify tangible Black and Indigenous History and Equity in Venice, California."[11]

"As African-Americans, Africa will always be our motherland," writes Los Angeles resident Jeremy Divinity. "Still, we don't have a direct connection to the continent and were stripped of our people's history. But what we do know is right there next to the beach. It's all we have. In a way, our motherland is Oakwood."[12]

Whitewashing the Walls

"So it is better to speak / remembering / we were never meant to survive."

—Audre Lorde

Hundreds of miles to the north, another cultural landmark became a focal point of resistance. José Meza's Mural de la Raza adorned a Payless Shoe Source at King and Story roads in a Chicanx neighborhood on San José's East Side. The mural, featuring Chicanx and Mexican historical icons to the side of an Aztec pyramid, provided a canvas for graffiti artists and united rival neighborhoods when it went up in the 1980s.

"This mural saved lives," writes J. M. Valle. "The Mural de La Raza was my mirror, and pulled my heart into the books that my public school teachers dared not to touch."[13]

Amidst rising property values, the Payless was shuttered and sold in 2018. That fall, community members awoke to find the historic mural had been painted over in the middle of the night. The wall was covered in gray paint save for a small portion depicting the Virgin of Guadalupe. Soon, the Virgin was painted over, too.[14] As in Venice, the physical obliteration of a cultural monument provided a rallying point for a community fighting gentrification. "During the past 15 years, there has been a chain of Chicano Murals that have been tragically removed, largely due to redevelopment and gentrification," per Valle. "But without any Chicano families with generational connections to our murals, murals start disappearing without anyone to defend them. I too can no longer afford to live back home in East Side San Jo."[15]

Meza filed a $5 million lawsuit against the building owners for a violation of the Visual Artists Rights Act, a federal law that requires that muralists be notified before their work is removed. The destruction of the Mural de la Raza inspired the creation of El Emergency Comité for the Preservation of Chicano Arts and multiple mass demonstrations at the site.[16]

The whitewashing of the mural formed a powerful, immediate reference point for the whitewashing of a community, connecting displacement, over-policing, and cultural erasure. "People tried to highlight those connections" to the concurrent campaign against the San José Google development, says Vasudha, "but I don't think we successfully managed to get that message across."[17]

Bryan Peraza organized against the Google campus while a student at San José State University before returning to fight displacement in his hometown of Santa Ana. Peraza said that Santa Ana was once known to outsiders as the ghetto of Orange County, with "a bunch of gang members and a bunch of Mexicans."[18]

"Ten, fifteen years ago, it would be really rare to see any young white folks in Santa Ana. When I told people I lived there, it had such a negative connotation. Now, the same people who were hesitant to go a few years ago now go on the weekends because of the bars, festivals, and community events," says Jenna, who grew up in Orange County before her family moved to the High Desert because of housing costs. For over two decades, private developments, public-private partnerships, and government infrastructure investments have radically changed Santa Ana into a city now seen as a hip and relatively inexpensive destination for artists, professionals, and university students.[19]

"A lot of art that's happening in downtown, it's out-of-state artists. They don't live here. There's so many talented queer, Latinx, brown people who are local and could be taking advantage of these opportunities, but gentrifiers will bring people from other states. Our community is constantly under attack because the city just sees us as the next Downtown LA," says David Carbajal Torres, a tenant organizer also born and raised in Santa Ana.[20]

Though cautioning against the risk of co-optation and tokenization, Peraza likewise views cultural projects as potentially significant vectors for resistance, especially in a community like Santa Ana where it can be obstructed by immigration status, language, and religious conservatism. He believes cultural projects can unite Santaneros, half of whom are born outside the US, predominantly in Mexico. "It's important to start there because we already have it," he said. "We already have a language, the music, the food, the culture and everything."

One lightning rod was the plan to turn a local supermarket into luxury condominiums. "The only days I've been there where it's empty have been New Year's or Christmas days. It's super small but it's always, always busy. My mom goes often because she knows the prices, the folks speak Spanish, the decor's very Mexican oriented," Peraza says. "The city as a whole is going to feel it because it's going to take something that made Santa Ana feel like it was for Latino folks and Santaneros." In an area without a strong history of grassroots organizing, culture provides a unifying force, a dividing line between a largely working-class Mexican community and the forces of redevelopment.

"When I see people bumping corridos down Flower Street, that to me is a way of fighting our oppression," says Carbajal Torres. "Every day, we meet señoras when we're canvassing, we start talking about rent control and then in a few minutes we're talking shit on cops. Our community knows. They don't have the academic language for it but they know: these are the conditions that we're in and they're not right. That they could live in a world where that doesn't exist. And that's what keeps us going, knowing that our people know, that our señoras know, and they're the backbone of our community."[21]

Formal oppositional organizing doesn't have a long history in Santa Ana. A radical analysis nonetheless prevails, though not constrained within a radical clique. To build resistance out of what "our people know" already, as Carbajal Torres puts it, Bryan Peraza emphasizes that "we can't just make our events serious—we need to make them fun. I look to movements in Latin America for inspiration. A lot of them have music and chanting. They're borderline parades, they're inviting, they're fun. We need a not-so-serious political approach to deal with these overly serious political issues that we have in our community."

In Mexico City, artists and activists in Colonia Juárez created Santa Mari la Juarica, patron saint of the local anti-gentrification struggle.[22] "Free me from displacement, from eviction, from rent and property tax increases, from the greedy landlord," goes a prayer created along with the saint in 2017. "Save me from gentrification."[23]

It is said that Saint Mari has already interceded to stop evictions and ensure the cancellation of the Corredor Cultural Chapultepec, a massive tree-lined elevated park planned along Avenida Chapultepec. Marketed as way to "recover" and "give back" an abandoned area to pedestrians, "recovering its history" while providing access to green spaces and cultural activities, the Cultural Corridor would have taken the form of a green outdoor mall, a "commercial corridor with restaurants and stores of a certain level, with the deteriorated zone remaining underneath as an underworld," in the words of Kanahuati from the Comité Ciudadano San Ángel.[24]

47

Communities around the world have successfully resisted dispersal through mobilizing the social ties that make such dispersal so painful. In San José, anti-gentrification groups held rent parties inspired by the Harlem Renaissance events, sharing food and dancing to live music before the door money was raffled off to a random attendee to cover their rent for the month. Berlin residents organized over cakes and coffee at a biweekly Anti-Google Café in an anarchist library.[25] Social ties, cultural practices, and common knowledges might all be weapons in defense of home, so long as they are turned against the enemy.

The Price of Memory

"A lot of things totaled in my mind, mostly that this society puts property before people, some sick motherfuckers are at the controls, and the very fate of humanity is at stake.

"Now just this knowledge and no knowledge of how to deal with this shit has driven a lot of people crazy."

—*Kuwasi Balagoon*

Mass displacement appropriates housing while excising home. "Housing" is an abstraction, the abstract equivalent of a rented bunk bed and a luxury loft. Housing might be anywhere. One's home is not. It is the memories, the textures, the meanings that have made up a life. If all those who know a place are removed, the place itself is no more, no matter how many buildings may yet remain.

"A lot of folks have built a life here with family, friends, and community," says San José's Daniel González. "Gentrification reveals the fragility of all that and really drives home the fact that we are, under present-day conditions, at the mercy of the local government and capitalism."[26] A gentrifying neighborhood sees its social networks torn apart as their members are dispersed to different places. The fight to retain a culturally significant place like a church or a mural can counteract that centrifugal motion by drawing together those under threat of displacement, those whose families have already been pushed out, and sometimes those who otherwise wouldn't have a stake in the fight. All three of these elements were at play in the fight for the Venice church, where people with past family ties to the area and historical preservationists joined together with current Oakwood residents.

When a given location becomes a communally significant place, the "concretion of value" collectively invested in it is never purely economic.[27] A building, landmark, meeting place, or piece of art is significant to its community by virtue of its history, legacy, or popular recognition, not its price tag. The building owners who whitewashed the Mural de la Raza in San José claimed that no prospective buyer would close the deal on the property unless the mural was first destroyed. If this is true, the mural's economic value was negative, though the land upon which it stood now came at a premium.

The destruction of a neighborhood landmark for profit provides a stark demonstration of community erasure. It can serve as a focal point to pull together resistance against a process tearing a community apart. And just like a "housing crisis" unfolding in front of vacant luxury condos, a "life-saving mural" being appraised as an economic liability lays bare the unresolvable tension between community survival and capitalist logic.

A mural is "not just the belonging of that property owner, but it becomes something that belongs to the community," said Elisa Marina Alvarado, who invited Mexican artist Gustavo Bernal Navarro to paint one at a San José health clinic.[28] A piece of art commonly recognized as belonging to a community is at risk of destruction because, per the courts and cops, it's actually the property of a building owner who may have never laid eyes on it in their life. A fight for culture unfolds into a fight over communal as opposed to capitalist ownership, an implicit or explicit critique of market exchange itself.

"There's exchange-value, and there's use-value. And we know

that exchange value has gotten us in the place where we are," says Oakland's Noni Session, director of the East Bay Permanent Real Estate Cooperative. "So decommodifying land reminds us of the right usage of a roof and a door and a window and ground upon which to stand. The right usage is to ground community and to ground the future."[29]

Representation as Weapon

"There's a way in which the process of memorialization is sometimes the first step in collective forgetting."

—Leigh Raiford

As in the case of the Corredor Cultural Chapultepec, the cultural legacies attached to a community's home can also be appropriated by the very institutions that are destroying it. Cultural preservation and representation are a nexus of resistance when they are part of a contention for power. But preservation and representation can also be offered to a community as a substitute for power and survival by those profiting from its destruction. Accepting some piece of commemoration in place of total oblivion is not unreasonable. But the danger is endorsing a memorial to one's own removal. "Beautiful! How beautiful! But it's somewhere only for those who are not like us," says a boy in tattered rags in one of Baudelaire's poems.[30] In the words of Mike Davis, "When it comes to the reclamation of high-value land, ideological symbols and promises made to the poor mean very little to the bureaucrats in power."[31]

Almost two years after selling public land to Google for a massive urban tech campus, the government of San José sponsored a local nonprofit hosting a "Community Visioning Workshop for Artists and Creatives" to manage popular opposition to the project.

The workshop's recorded notes dutifully reflect the assembled artists' wishes that development respect the cultural diversity of the area.[32]

Santa Ana's 4th Street, La Cuatro, has been a thriving Mexican commercial district since the 1970s.[33] But Western wear stores, quinceañera halls, and discount clothing stores are now replaced by microbreweries and vegan cafés marketed for artists, professionals, and university students. There are new Mexican restaurants on La Cuatro as well, but they target an Anglo clientele. "A lot of the staple stores that were in La Cuatro, they've been replaced by businesses that cater to different people. Restaurants use Spanish vocabulary, some have a Spanish, Mexican aesthetic, but it's not catering to the Spanish-speaking population," says Bryan Peraza. "You might have Spanish in the name or a few Spanish words in their menu, but the rest of the menu language isn't in Spanish." As Santa Ana gentrifies, a Mexican population is priced out as an outward-facing representation of Mexican culture grows.

In 2022, the Mexico City government announced a partnership with Airbnb and UNESCO to brand the metropolis as the "Capital of Creative Tourism" and launch a training program to "help entrepreneurs develop authentic cultural experiences" for remote workers and tourists.[34] "Digital nomads" will be able to consume such "uniquely Mexican" offerings when not patronizing the coffee shops and yoga studios sprouting up to meet their demand.[35]

In Philadelphia, a neighborhood association and historical preservation society rallied to preserve the buildings of Doctors' Row, which, in the early-twentieth century, served as the "Main Street for Philadelphia's Black Elite," a "million-dollar avenue" for the city's "colored wealth." Today, as its historic townhomes face demolition to make way for new condominiums, residents and preservationists have clamored for Doctors' Row to be protected as a historic district, "the first space in Philadelphia to receive that honor specifically for Black history."[36]

Doctors' Row sits within the Graduate Hospital neighborhood, whose Black population plummeted as it became the most affluent section of the city. The historic district would protect the Black history of an area that now possesses "the air of a freshly-minted '60s subdivision" with the addition of "hip cafes."[37] The director of a local jazz history project, Faye Anderson, views the preservation campaign for the now-majority-white area as less a victory for racial justice than an attempt by white property owners to increase the value of their new homes. "The proposed historic district trivializes Black history in an effort to preserve the historic fabric of blocks from which African Americans have been displaced," she writes.[38] A memorial to Black history may serve as the capstone to Black exclusion. "All that was once directly lived has become mere representation."[39] What is represented—made re-present, present once again—must be made absent first.

Know Your Enemy

"We are who we are / To them, even when we don't know who we / Are to each other & culture is a / Record of us figuring that out."

—*Wendy Trevino*

James Baldwin writes that he "spent most of my life, after all, watching white people and outwitting them, so that I might survive."[40] The oppressed must be able to think from the perspective of the oppressor in order to navigate the world, while the privileged have no compulsion to adopt the perspective of anyone else.[41] American media corporations broadcast the lives of wealthy and middle-class white Americans all over the world, but poor communities of color remain threateningly inscrutable to the affluent enclaves next door. The local knowledges of those dwelling in specific places are invisible and unprofitable to newcomers or the investors standing behind them. A neighborhood must be made legible to prospective residents before it is marketed to them. A Santa Ana taquería might be illegible in the most literal sense, the items on its Spanish-language menu not only unfamiliar but incomprehensible to English speakers.

Modern states not only map their territories to make sense of them but also, as James C. Scott argues, remake reality to conform with their maps. Perfectly square plots of land are drawn up before their boundaries are enforced at gunpoint. A neighborhood is demolished so its roads can be rebuilt on an orderly, police-friendly grid. Subjects are affixed permanent surnames to track and tax them throughout their lives. The violence of governance requires legibility; the maintenance of legibility requires governance. From this perspective, legibility becomes a "central problem in statecraft."[42] And for a poor district to become an "up-and-coming neighborhood," it must make sense to developers, investors, planners, and the white-collar workers who will one day call it home.[43] While the unknown might conceal disorder and danger, what is visible may be policed. What is recognizable may be advertised.

The taming of New York's Union Square Park in the 1980s included the removal of trees and the creation of open areas for "long-range visibility for surveillance and control."[44] Benches were redesigned so unhoused people couldn't sleep on them. The Tompkins Square Park bandshell, where the New York chapter of the Young Lords Party announced their formation in 1969, was demolished to dispel squatters and activists, though only after years of riotous resistance.[45]

The gentrifying residential neighborhood is often renamed as it acquires amenities that its new residents will be comfortable consuming. San Francisco real estate agent Jennifer Rosdail embarked on a lonely quest to rename the Mission District as "the Quad." One of the city's oldest neighborhoods, the Mission is the site of fierce community resistance to new luxury housing developments. But the Quad, per Rosdail, is a hip locale perfectly suited to young techies who "make a lot of money." "You may hate 'gentrification,'" she writes, "but Quadsters like the mix of lux and grit."[46]

Los Angeles city government tried to rid South Central of associations with crime and urban rebellion by renaming it "South Los Angeles" through legislative fiat in 2003. Developers intend to rebrand a chunk of Harlem as "SoHa" and rechristen the South

Bronx as the "Piano District."⁴⁷ In Oakland, Northgate became Koreatown-Northgate, then KONO, while the Lower Bottoms became Prescott.⁴⁸ A real estate company attempted to disguise San Francisco's Tenderloin neighborhood as Union Square West.⁴⁹

Conducted by or at the behest of "big business with little or no personal connection to the places they rename," these changes are met with confusion or revulsion by many of the people who live there, who were neither consulted nor informed.⁵⁰ There was no reason to: it is not them but their replacements who are the intended audience. If the common name of a neighborhood shifts to the new one dreamed up by a corporate marketing department, it is not through popular adoption but through coerced replacement. The residents of Harlem are priced out; the residents of SoHa move in.

The customary names of exploited urban areas might carry any number of connotations, rightly or wrongly deserved, for privileged outsiders: criminality, danger, foreignness, or, as geographer Neil Smith identifies, the recurrent, genocidal imagery of the untamed frontier. A place invented *ex nihilo* is weighed down by none of these burdens, only by the legacy community whose existence impedes its full manifestation.

West Philadelphia's working-class Black neighborhood of the Black Bottom sat in the path of Drexel and the University of Pennsylvania as their enrollments swelled after World War II. The construction of the nation's first urban research park displaced thousands of Black residents as the neighborhood was rechristened "University City" and redeveloped as a "*cordon sanitaire* in the Market Street corridor that would buffer Penn from the blight and crime . . . [that] the city planners of that era associated with the low-income, Black-majority neighborhoods to the north and west of the campus."⁵¹ While the name "Black Bottom" begs the question of where so many Black families have gone, the "University City" label, invented by developers to attract faculty members in the 1950s, only points to university-related development not yet completed.[52]

"The Black Bottom is not in University City. The university is in the Black Bottom," say former residents, dozens of whom gather for Black Bottom Tribe reunions each year.[53] Darlene Foreman, born and raised in the Black Bottom, now lives in the original neighborhood's "last standing property," a seventy-unit Section 8 subsidy housing development called the University City Townhomes.[54] Foreman and her neighbors launched a protracted fight against the property owners, Altman Management, who seek to evict the residents and redevelop the site as market-rate housing.[55]

"They took everything from 32nd Street all the way around to the hospital over to here. This is the last property. Penn and Drexel, they just took it. They moved people out, they did whatever they needed to do to take all of that property," says Foreman. Demanding that the property be taken off the market and removed from Altman's ownership, the residents now call the University City Townhomes the People's Townhomes. Renaming locations as a weapon in neighborhood transformation can be wielded by communities in resistance as it is by developers and politicians.

Power and Vacations

"I once started out / to walk around the world / but ended up in Brooklyn."

—*Lawrence Ferlinghetti*

University of Pennsylvania alumni have access to Penn Alumni Travel tours, exclusive opportunities to visit Alsace, Egypt, or the Iberian Peninsula in the refined company of other Penn graduates. The politics of place and displacement follow gentrifiers on holiday, as well. Depending on the balance of class interests and power, the unique character of a place can attract gentrification as much as it can be wielded as a weapon against it. Charming Barcelona's tourist-centered redevelopment started in earnest during preparation for the 1992 Olympics and intensified when the Convergència i Unió party rezoned swathes of the city to attract international capital in the depths of the Great Recession.[56] Today, Barcelona has reached an "acute" state of gentrification thanks to the appeal of its "historical heritage, cultural dynamism, business economy," and beaches.[57] "The neighbors are disappearing," reported one resident, saying rents had increased by two hundred Euros in recent years. "They are leaving." But tourism is now a "fundamental industry," per the managing partner of a hospitality consulting firm. "Many directly or indirectly connected industries would suffer greatly without it."[58]

With Airbnb, landlords around the world can easily replace tenants with tourists, multiplying the amount of money they receive each month. A San Francisco landlord evicted a tenant paying $1,840 a month to charge tourists twice as much.[59] Airbnb rentals are estimated to have raised average rents in New York City by $400 a year.[60] The platform has faced pushback in cities from Amsterdam to Venice as housing units are reserved for globe-trotting tourists.[61]

This tourism gentrification, which carves up working-class neighborhoods to attract vacationers' dollars with hotels, resorts, restaurants, and shopping districts, is less frequently discussed in the United States, perhaps because the nation's intellectuals and academics find themselves partaking in the practice on holiday. The international vacation destination ought to be foreign and exceptional—nothing less justifies the airfare. But it must also make sense to the vacationer. There must be appealing hotels easily booked, attractions advertised in an understandable way, staff who speak their language, restaurants with menus that fit their tastes. As Guy Debord pointed out, tourism is "the opportunity to go and see what has been banalized," commodified, made legible and essentially equivalent to any other vacation destination one might choose.[62]

The fully engineered tourist district attracts huge amounts of foreign capital that can anchor the economy of an entire region or nation. Land was legally bought and sold in post-revolutionary Cuba for the first time in 2011.[63] Though non-Cubans are formally excluded from the market, it is reported that many property sales are funded with remittances from Cuban American relatives or conducted by Cuban citizens operating at the behest of foreign buyers.[64]

Almost two decades before the establishment of a real estate market, the Cuban state began emphasizing tourism as a way to attract foreign capital. In the early 1980s, several buildings in Old Havana were recognized as UNESCO World Cultural Heritage

sites—a designation supposed to recognize the objective importance and international legibility of a place while facilitating
economic and technical assistance for historic restoration. During
the economic devastation of the post-Soviet "Special Period," when
petroleum imports to the island virtually ceased, the state developed public institutions to promote tourism while dilapidated
colonial buildings were transformed from residential units into
restaurants and luxury hotels. Former residents were directly displaced to the city's outskirts.[65] Even while the ban on real estate
speculation remained, the increased valuation of Old Havana real
estate was expressed in the informal market. Remaining tenants
began renting out rooms or running small businesses that ben-
efitted from easy access to the tourist market. (Access to foreign
currency is so significant that Cuban taxi drivers can make more
than surgeons.) In 2001, 40 percent of residences were free tene-
ments; by 2019, it was only 12 percent, with 75 percent of residences
in touristified Old Havana now private property.[66] If privatization
and tourism-oriented redevelopment is the priority of a state whose
foundational narrative is the revolutionary expropriation of private property, it should be no surprise when US state elites find
economic incentives more convincing than purported liberal commitments to "inclusion," "diversity," or "the community."[67]

On Camps

"I believe in life. / And i have seen the death parade / march through the torso of the earth, / sculpting mud bodies in its path."

—*Assata Shakur*

Domestically, the new economy has birthed a perverse symmetry, one wrought in social and physical death. While the winners of the gentrification economy are concentrated in *campuses*, those most oppressed are concentrated in so-called *encampments*: the informal, illegal communities of the unhoused who have been priced out of housing but remain in the urban core. The shocking growth of unhoused communities is the direct effect of the same economic polarization that drives displacement away from the city.

And in a second symmetry, while the concentration camp is the site where the state makes everything comprehensible to itself, the niceties of legal personhoods, identities, and rights replaced by identification numbers and the unrestricted administration of death, the unhoused "encampment" threatens the state and capital with its opacity to those who don't dare to enter but would still presume to govern.[68]

A perennial myth holds that a majority of unhoused people in certain cities moved there to access generous social services. This suggests that the best way to reduce homelessness in an area is to decrease the amount of homeless services available. In actuality, the majority of those unhoused in any area are inevitably formerly housed local residents.[69] Per the US Governmental Accountability Office, a $100 rise in the median rent of an area is associated with a 9 percent increase in homelessness—hardly a correlation that suggests that overabundant service provision is to blame.[70]

"Nobody actually wants to be homeless, to live in a shelter, or have the problems that they have," says ACT UP Philadelphia's Jazmyn. "It's our social and economic system that creates this problem."[71] ACT UP Philly grew its fight for HIV treatment into a struggle for housing, given that houselessness is a major risk factor for contracting HIV and losing access to treatment. ACT UP targeted Philadelphia's Office of Homeless Services with the demand that a board of currently unhoused people oversee the department's policies.

Local elites sponsor the dispersal, not concentration, of unhoused populations, as tent cities and visible destitution are both the result of and a brake on further redevelopment. "There used to be a lot of encampments of unhoused folks in the beach cities like Huntington and Newport. They would literally bus them into Santa Ana and Anaheim because it was an 'eyesore,'" says Jenna from Santa Ana. New York City buys unhoused families one-way airplane tickets to the local or international destination of their choice. "We have paid for visas, we've gone down to the consulate, we've provided letters, we've paid for passports for people to go," says an official quoted in a 2009 article.[72] Half of the unhoused people taken off the streets of San Francisco are simply put on a Greyhound out of town; most never find housing.[73] The perverse justification for such programs is the false notion that those shipped away were all from out of town to begin with.[74]

State violence against unhoused "encampments" should remind us that the very terminology is military. It is soldiers, those engaged in one side of a martial conflict, who occupy encampments by the field of battle.

"There was at least 300 to 400 people living underneath the 580 freeway, which I would call a neighborhood, because that's what it is, or maybe a small town. I don't use the military-industrial-complex notion of 'encampment,'" says Lisa "Tiny" Gray-García, a member of a Bay Area collective of currently and formerly unhoused activists, artists, and scholars called POOR Magazine/Prensa POBRE.[75] "It takes the humanity away from it. That's why they use that word. It comes out of the military."

Tiny says that the people under the freeway "started their own free food delivery, free stores. They would help people with clothes if they didn't have them. They would have a little safe haven place for people to sit and get healed with different massage techniques. All houseless folks, and some housed folks who would throw down in a real way."

The strategy of politicians and developers is often to play the interests of precarious tenants against the currently unhoused. The police and property developers pretend to be the allies of tenants in "cleaning up" the neighborhood, though the average tenant is far closer to becoming unhoused themselves than they are to becoming a police sergeant or real estate CEO. Connecting the material and physical defense of unhoused communities with the defense of tenants—those from whom rent is extracted through the threat that they might be made unhoused—is one way to construct an oppositional bloc.

ACT UP Philly is focusing on Kensington, a gentrifying Black neighborhood with large numbers of people on the streets amidst a thriving drug market. The drug trade and number of visibly unhoused people slow rising property values, with capitalists and the state responding accordingly.

"Every place they have swept an encampment out of Kensington has been gentrified. If you go to where an encampment was, they're building a bunch of high-rise condos," says Jazmyn Henderson of ACT UP Philly. "They convinced the residents of Kensington that they need to get rid of the homeless people to have higher property values, but I promise you: as soon as they clear all the homeless people off the streets of Kensington, what you're going to see is a bunch of new developments being built at a price you can't afford."[76]

There have always been those whose existence is of so little utility to the owning class that those owners find protecting them from the elements an unnecessary expense. But the magnitude of houselessness in the contemporary United States and the profit-ability of mass expulsion—even during economic boom times, and especially from those cities with the most wealth—is a recent phenomenon. It was not until the rich spread their shopping districts and campuses that the poor were commonly reduced to "encampments."

"The tech industry started out here with a lot of chip factories and a lot of production actually happened here, but that was almost all outsourced in the 1980s," says Sandy Perry. "The tech industry in San José became pretty much only research and development and design. All the production was done in China. What you had here was deindustrialization and this really rapid polarization of wealth and poverty. People's wages went down, their standard of living went down. . . . That was the beginning of the era when you have lot of homeless people in San José."[77]

III. LABOR

"The urban fabric, with its multiple networks of communication and exchange, is part of the means of production. The city and its various installations (ports, train stations, etc.) are part of capital."

—*Henri Lefebvre*

In April 2018, as the clandestine pellet gun assailant still menaced the windows of local Google buses, dozens rallied outside San Francisco City Hall to oppose the loosening of state zoning restrictions. The rally was disrupted when a "vitriolic" group of largely white California YIMBY members descended, shouting down speakers and aggressively confronting a mostly Black, brown, and Asian group of community members concerned about displacement. Sonja Trauss, a regional leader of the "Yes in My Backyard" (YIMBY) pro-development movement, charged to the front to wave her sign in the face of a Chinese elder. Another elder from Chinatown's Community Tenants Association fainted and was hospitalized. Association president Wing Hoo Leung described it as the worst counter-protest he'd seen in fifteen years of organizing.[1]

Per YIMBY proponents, the obvious solution to the high cost of housing is the construction of more of it. People in a working-class neighborhood may think they oppose new luxury condominiums, say the YIMBYs, but insofar as they want lower rents, they actually want the opposite.[2] Such vitriol as was on display at the April counter-rally is thus often fueled by a sneering condescension drawn from the idea that only those without "a basic understanding of economics" could oppose YIMBY principles.[3] To the YIMBY mind, those grandparents outside city hall were the irrational victims of their own naïveté and ignorance. This arrogance is undoubtedly enriched by the fact that a disproportionate number of YIMBY advocates come from a tech world whose members sometimes imagine themselves as a "cognitive elite."[4]

Everything else being equal, a commodity becoming more plentiful should cause its price to drop. The idea that increasing the supply of housing will decrease its cost accordingly has a common sensical, Econ 101 sort of appeal. That such a rudimentary understanding of supply and demand is not actually sufficient to explain the world, much less justify shouting down immigrant grandparents, is proven by, among other things, the existence of Econ 201.

In one article purporting to prove that luxury housing development is actually good for the poor, California YIMBY's Sonja Trauss is forced to assume that the amount of housing has no influence on housing demand, that landlords would potentially rent any unit at any price whatsoever, that each isolated tenant has no housing preferences beyond how objectively "nice" (on a scale from one to five) she would like her housing to be, and that each and every tenant across San Francisco is equally able to fairly bid for whichever unit she might prefer. With enough abstractions, Trauss triumphantly concludes that the construction of two thousand luxury units will cause two thousand fewer people to be displaced.[5]

Around the United States, such new luxury housing often comes in the form of the boxy multistory buildings known as the "5-over-1." Designed to minimize construction costs and maximize floor space within the constraints of building codes, such constructions are particularly profitable for the redeveloper.[6] (They are also particularly flammable.)[7] Their expansion across the urban landscape is a concrete marker of the capital poured into neighborhoods to attract wealthier residents. But opposition to the march of the 5-over-1s is described by YIMBYs as a mere "aesthetic" disinclination if not sheer ignorance. "It is fine to dislike the way a home looks; not all art is for everyone," writes Jerusalem Demsas for *Vox*. But associating them with displacement because of uninformed "confusion" is entirely self-defeating, she continues, since cheap new construction will obviously lower housing prices. Those too uninformed to realize such elementary truths fight "the very policies necessary to solve the nation's affordability crisis."[8]

5-over-1 "gentrification buildings" in Madison, Wisconsin, raised the price of surrounding units as soon as their permits were issued. Over half a year, nearby evictions increased by 60.7 percent.[9] Areas of Chicago upzoned to incentivize new construction became more valuable, not less expensive.[10] In Minneapolis, Minnesota, new market-rate developments caused the price of nearby luxury units to drop—but caused rent for adjacent cheaper units to rise.[11] An analysis of the San Francisco Bay Area reported that the rich "disproportionately benefit from new market-rate housing production."[12] The smug self-assuredness of the YIMBY lobby is simply unjustified, as is their conviction that tenants' opposition to more market-rate construction results from some sort of elementary failure to understand economic laws.

"Most cities go above and beyond their goals for market-rate housing. Still, not everyone has access to those homes," says Liz González. "The whole statement about us not having enough housing is a myth. We just don't have the kind of housing that meets people's needs, that is affordable, because the market-rate housing is out of reach for almost everyone."[13]

"Santa Ana has development and they're not being filled," says David Carbajal Torres. "People cannot afford to live in them. More housing does not equal more opportunities for people to live in it."[14]

It remains the case that, in most gentrifying cities, it is virtually impossible to find "reputable" sources on how many people have been displaced. We are left on one hand with the "objectivity" of rising median incomes and better-performing schools, and on the other with the "anecdotal" evidence of thousands of working-class people, mostly people of color, about how their lives and communities have been torn apart. The Richmond Federal Reserve published an evidently non-satirical paper touting the benefits to be had if half the population of San José were to pack up and move to Las Vegas.[15] We are told that our displacement is good: for the community, for the city, for ourselves. The YIMBY line is that the communities fighting displacement in fact make it worse while the real estate developers who profit from gentrification are the only ones who can put it to an end.

The name YIMBY comes from NIMBY, Not In My Backyard, a label for someone who selfishly opposes a new development, social service, or industry solely because it would be located inconveniently nearby. The pejorative may be attached to anyone from a suburban homeowner frightened of a new apartment building's prospective tenants of color to the working-class Chinese elders chanting under the California sun. But not all housing is created equal, and neither are the people housed. No quantity of sublet bedrooms will satisfy the professional seeking a luxury condominium, and the contemporary city government finds scores of precarious laborers a poor substitute for a handful of software engineers.

"You might think that building housing will raise the supply, and the laws of economics tell us that prices will go down. But is the new housing only affordable for a certain class of people? Is any of it earmarked for low-income people or seniors? There's a differential in the type of housing that's being built. You have to look at what the target market really is," explains Vasudha.[16] The YIMBY narrative erases the question of power between privileged and expendable workers and between landlords and tenants to pose gentrification as the result of a simple technical problem: a numerical deficit in the absolute number of housing units because of market constraints. This analysis is welcomed by developers on the hunt for building permits and tech firms looking to house their employees.

"When we call this crisis a housing crisis, it benefits the people who design housing, who build housing, who profit from housing, not the people who live in it," writes Tracy Rosenthal of the LA Tenants Union. "We don't have a housing crisis. We have a tenants' rights crisis."[17]

The Union's Inspiration

"The working class has always created the organizational tools to wage its battles."

—*Selma James*

A few months after the YIMBYs advocated for low-income tenants by shouting them down in public, professional tech workers from Square and Google joined an Apple subcontractor and an Uber driver at a San Francisco meeting of the Tech Workers Coalition. Techies and contractors alike convened to learn labor law and unite in proletarian solidarity. After all, one of the trainers announced, "a worker is a worker," one and all. "In our perfect world," said a Tech Workers Coalition organizer, "we'd have Uber drivers working with Uber engineers, fighting together," having stripped away the veil of ideology to fight the class struggle side by side.[18]

This meeting occurred in the Mission District, a place where a class struggle surely raged, though not one in which software engineers and gig workers came together against the capitalist class. The struggle against urban displacement pits the interests of low-wage workers and unemployed people against high-paid gentrifiers. It is therefore forced to confront the changing configurations of production under late capitalism.

The Tech Workers Coalition includes Google employees who

loudly protested the development of artificial intelligence for military drones and walked out after the creator of Android received $90 million for being terminated for sexual harassment. Their mission is to remind other tech workers that they, too, are wage laborers, although perhaps temporarily confused by Silicon Valley meritocratic ideas and their comfortable work environments. Since "tech workers are workers, too," when highly paid engineers support unionizing cafeteria workers, it is simply solidarity between two segments of the same working class. To fight against their shared exploitation by their employers, "the workers must realize their class position and exercise their class power."[19]

Organized workers can and should demand that their employers stop objectionable practices outside the workplace as well as within it. The question is why organizations of left-leaning techies should be considered unions rather than progressive internal pressure groups. While it's true that by virtue of their positions, tech professionals have particular leverage against the tech firms that employ them, labor unions primarily struggle to improve the material conditions of work for workers.[20] There's good reason to wonder whether union campaigns for high-paid software engineers are even unions at all.

Though tech workers are workers insofar as they go to work at companies that they do not own, they aren't workers to the degree that a large portion of their benefits are stock options in those companies, meaning they have a direct financial stake in their employers' profits. It is in their material interest to wrest more money, time, and decision-making power from their bosses, but both employer and employee have an interest in the ultimate success of the company's stock prices (and not merely, as in the case of all workers, in the survival of the firm and its generation of profits sufficient to provide for a hypothetical wage increase). Both tech executives and their direct employees also benefit from gentrification that's designed to turn more of the city into an environment optimized for their convenience and consumption. The gulf between the material interests and strategic potentialities of the well-off tech worker, the café barista, the pre-revolutionary Russian foundry worker, and the undocumented slaughterhouse laborer covered in viscera can't be narrowed by describing how each partakes of the same substance, "worker." This reduces working-class politics to a politics of identity in the crudest way: "the representation of the working class has become an enemy of the working class."[21]

The Workers' Blood

"Revolutionary workers: Cultivate disrespect."
—*Ricardo Flores Magón*

In October 2020, *Philadelphia Magazine* published an article on the city's "new generation of unions." Above a picture of earnest, fair-skinned socialists posing in an abandoned building, we are told of efforts to organize a gentrifier bakery called Cake Life. It is not until the last section of the article that we learn that the result of such efforts was that Cake Life was shuttered and all of its employees fired. "It just drives home the need," a laid-off employee tells us, amazingly, "for this sort of organizing."[22]

The article was published three days after protestors gathered across the United States to mark what would have been George Floyd's forty-seventh birthday as the largest social uprising in the nation's history tapered off.[23] Its lesson for workers, per the author, is that "protest, which is to say organizing, works." The only issue is that in the case of Cake Life, it didn't.

The days in which any large American union sought revolutionary changes in production have long passed. Today's business unions use the same managerial toolbox as the companies on the other side of the negotiating table. Working-class power is not on the agenda, and workers themselves often play a marginal role in the whole process. Union staff instead represent members' narrow economic interests by advocating for higher wages and better benefits, sometimes negligibly so.[24] Devoting resources to organize a single small business is a poor investment for a traditional labor union given the small amount of dues they would receive from union members in return. The word "investment" is not accidental.

The unions that by and large refuse to help small workplaces organize are undemocratic and reformist. Their ideological and legal commitments are toward securing increased economic benefits for new and existing members, if anything, not promoting worker resistance in general. This leads to the belief among some radical unionists that mainstream unions refuse to organize small workplaces *only because* they are undemocratic and reformist, and that a lack of revolutionary vigor, and perhaps little else, is therefore the chief obstacle to organizing the small workplaces of the contemporary US service economy.

The closure of Cake Life could be the result of a terrified capitalist class rushing to cut off worker militancy at the root lest the laboring masses reclaim their surest weapons, the union and the strike. More likely, it was the result of a pragmatic decision by the owners upon realizing that their bakery would no longer be competitive in a sea of other gentrifier eateries should they be forced to pay union wages.

With millions underwater in debt, we do not lack a mass workers movement for want of poverty. And in the wake of Occupy Wall Street, discussion of economic inequality and class have returned from the fringes of US political discourse, even if caged in social democratic terms that portray anti-capitalism as a matter of adjusting tax rates and health insurance payments. But in a fragmented economy where many work at small firms, there are numerous examples of labor actions that end not in revolution or even a raise but the owners cutting their losses and shutting down. In Philadelphia, this was the case not only at Cake Life but at two other restaurants, V Street and Good Karma Café, as well.[25] While large employers such as tech companies and universities accumulate clusters of privileged workers, those with an economic interest in uprooting the world of exploitation, dispossession, and labor often find themselves employed at an industrial patchwork of small restaurants, nursing homes, bars, and nail salons, if not working as independent contractors in the gig economy. To go on strike at a Manchester textile factory in the 1800s dealt a blow to the capitalist class; to strike at an independent restaurant in the Silicon Valley today is largely irrelevant to capitalism at large. Unionizing the steel works that form the heart of a regional economy is qualitatively different from unionizing a small business perched on its edge.

As San José's Daniel González puts it, "I really view what happened with my family as the reverse of industrialization. The reason there's not really a need for people like me or members of my family around is because it's more profitable to urbanize and do it with a certain type of individual, especially here in Silicon Valley. You know, tech workers and people who work in high-paying jobs."[26] The danger, under modern conditions, is to hew to the union form to signal fidelity to the class struggle of the historic left rather than investigate its use as a node in the class struggle around us.

Anywhere Beneath the Sun

"And was Jerusalem builded here / Among these dark
Satanic mills?"

—*William Blake*

Viewing class politics from the perspective of communities fighting displacement highlights the wildly divergent interests between two sectors of "workers" under a novel, "fully global mode of class-based sociospatial reorganization" that presents a mirror image of the distribution of factory workers under industrial capitalism.[27]

All social struggle takes place on the terrain of spatial distribution: the desires and understandings, sorrows and joys, and acts of resistance or complacence of persons with certain bodies inhabiting certain spaces. Their actions to reinforce or reject social structures also emanate from particular coordinates, whether a bottle thrown or a vote cast. Because of this, the forms and potentialities of resistance are always conditioned by the locations of those who would resist.

Simone de Beauvoir attributes deficits in feminist consciousness under patriarchy to the fact that women's spatial distribution among men disallows them a "concrete means of organizing themselves into a unit." Women are not "promiscuously herded together in the way that creates community feeling" like that between residents of a Black or Jewish ghetto or "the workers of Saint-Denis, or the factory hands of Renault."[28]

The theory that those herded-together workers and factory hands constitute the revolutionary class didn't drop from the sky. It emerged from the already-existing worker revolts of the nineteenth and twentieth centuries, revolts that allowed workers to "feel an identity of interests as between themselves, and as against their rulers and employers," and to vie for power as members of an "insurgent working class" once concentrated in the wealthiest cities of their day.[29]

The program of Mikhail Bakunin's International Brethren anticipates the social revolution spreading outward from the capital, which "is to declare itself in rebellion and organize itself as a Commune" before "an appeal will be issued to all provinces, communes and associations, inviting them to follow [its] example."[30] Peter Kropotkin's report to the Jura Federation, the anarchist successor the International Working Man's Association, similarly assumes that a revolutionary period of several years will be necessary to ensure "that the propagation of new ideas should not be confined solely to the great intellectual centers, but should reach even into the most isolated hamlets in order to shake the inertia which is necessarily evident in the masses prior to their turning towards a fundamental reorganization of society."[31]

As John Thelwall, the leader of the English Jacobins at the dawn of the Industrial Revolution, puts it: "Monopoly, and the hideous accumulation of capital in a few hands . . . carry in their own enormity, the seeds of cure. . . . Whatever presses men together . . . though it may generate some vices, is favourable to the diffusion of knowledge, and ultimately promotive of human liberty. Hence every large workshop and manufactory is a sort of political society, which no act of parliament can silence, and no magistrate disperse."[32]

79

The proletarian revolts of the industrial age occurred around large firms that concentrated masses of low-wage workers under conditions that facilitated worker organization and militancy. Ford, General Motors, and Chrysler Fiat were the giants of twentieth-century Detroit. The nineteenth-century development of the steam engine allowed Manchester to host cotton factories whose immensity gave "notice from afar of the centralization of industry," in the words of Alexis de Tocqueville.[33] They were "something new in the world": industry at an unprecedented scale.[34]

Bakunin's quote centering urban industrial revolt came two years before, and Kropotkin's several years after, the 1871 establishment of the Paris Commune. The insurrectionary capture of Paris was celebrated by anarchists as the abolition of the state and by Marx as the dictatorship of the proletariat—a "glorious harbinger of a new society."[35]

Today, the poor are dispersed not only spatially, through displacement, but also industrially, through an array of precarious service industry jobs and gig work. In place of the factories of Big Three automakers, we have the campuses of Big Five tech companies pulling workers together. Pittsburgh's steelworks have been replaced by medicine and finance. Chicago's meatpacking factories made way for insurance company offices. Milwaukee shed over fifty thousand manufacturing jobs in the three years after 1980, with shopping mall jobs paying half as much as the factory jobs they replaced.[36] Industry has fled the affluent city.

The broad category of "services" includes both poles of the gentrification economy, from store clerk to financial advisor. It now accounts for a majority of US GDP.[37] From 1994 to 2019, income for workers at large firms grew 25 percent quicker than it did for workers at firms with nineteen employees or less.[38] In the words of scholar Jean Anyon: "Large and small factories used to dot the downtowns of most large cities. Today, most neighborhoods in the central cities and urbanized low-income suburbs have bodegas, 'deli's' and other small businesses—and relatively few jobs, compared to the number that are needed."[39]

Contemporary urbanism, as Debord identifies, is "the modern method for solving the ongoing problem of safeguarding class power by atomizing the workers, who had been dangerously brought together by the conditions of urban production."[40] The factories that confronted de Tocqueville were followed by a Second Industrial Revolution of electrification and assembly line production at the turn of the twentieth century and a Third Industrial Revolution of digital technology from mid-century to the present day. The World Economic Forum informs us that now, with developments in artificial intelligence, biotechnology, and the Internet of Things, we stand at the cusp of a Fourth. Per founder Klaus Schwab, "inequality represents the greatest societal concern" of this latest transformation, with the "job market increasingly segregated into 'low skill/low pay' and 'high skill/high pay' segments." This segregation, he informs us, "will lead to an increase in social tensions."[41] Antigentrification fights in cities around the world show that these tensions are already upon us. Organizing at the point of production remains the response of some workers at critical locations within the new economy. But the context surrounding labor organizing has shifted with the reassignment of labor in the gentrification economy and the gentrifying cities it births.

In Common With the Greedy Parasite

"Without theoretical terrorism, there can be no revolution."
—*Alain Badiou*

In the spring of 2022, workers at Amazon's JFK8 warehouse on Staten Island made history by voting in the independent Amazon Labor Union. It was a significant victory not only because of the size of Amazon's consumer-facing operations, but also because employees defeated novel capitalist innovations designed to thwart worker organizing. Several weeks after the victory at JFK8, a smaller Staten Island warehouse rejected unionization by a wide margin.[42] And while Amazon employees organize warehouses, their nominal coworkers with advanced degrees rake in salaries starting at six figures from posh offices.

Warehouse work is a paradigmatic example of a traditional working-class job. But to cut off worker resistance in its international logistics network, Amazon employs a counter-intuitive management strategy. The company strives to meet goals for "unregretted attrition" of workers, achieving annual worker turnover at a rate twice the industry average. A "submit voluntary resignation" button is helpfully provided in the employee app.[43] The physical strain of keeping up with individualized, punishing production schedules sets what Italian union organizers call a "physiological" time limit on tenure, with the average warehouse worker lasting just three years.[44] Many are fired or quit within weeks.[45]

The brutality of such conditions is of course all the more incentive to organize at the point of the production, but fighting to improve a position I'll only work for a single holiday season is by design a tougher sell than taking risks to transform a job I'll be forced to work for decades or a lifetime. The Amazon warehouse produces a worker "contaminated by all characteristics of precariousness" through a model that "prevents the recognition of the existence of the working class at the very time its condition is spread."[46]

Amazon drivers are similarly expendable, expected to deliver packages as tornado warnings blare and relieve themselves in bottles over the course of sixteen-hour shifts.[47] Though their conditions are as bad and their careers often as short as their warehouse equivalents, drivers face the additional barrier of being employed through subcontractors, not by the company itself.[48] From one perspective, this is a pure legal fiction. Their formal employer, a company known as an Amazon Delivery Service Partner (DSP), uses Amazon-provided payroll software to compensate workers for driving Amazon-branded vans. The vans are leased from Amazon with Amazon-provided vehicle insurance programs and sent on Amazon-defined delivery routes through Amazon's navigation software, their locations tracked through Amazon package scanners.

While Amazon sets the conditions of work, it shifts risk onto Delivery Service Partner owners, "entrepreneurs" who launch "their own companies" with as little as a $10,000 investment and the completion of Amazon's training program. The company can easily drop their contract with an underperforming DSP and contract with another in its place. Owners have an incentive to break labor laws in pursuit of acceptable metrics but bear sole responsibility if these violations are discovered.[49]

This also means that the initial bargaining unit of a drivers' union would comprise the workers of a single subcontractor. Other drivers work for different employers, none of which are owned by Amazon. Any benefits won by the workers at a single Delivery Service Partner would evaporate as soon as Amazon dissolves its partnership.

The precarity of low-wage labor extends to Amazon's hulking corporate campus in Seattle. In 2017, the company held 19 percent of prime office space in the city, as much as the next forty largest employers combined.[50] In addition to direct, full-time employees, the Amazon campus is the workplace for the custodians who clean such areas as a whimsical Harry Potter-themed room complete with a miniature library, the groundskeepers who tend to the forty-foot trees that hold up the treehouse meeting spaces inside the massive glass Amazon Spheres, and the prep cooks working on the pickled purple cauliflower for the employee café's Creamy Saffron Cauliflower soup.[51]

Amazon benefits from competition between the national or multinational corporations it contracts out to for dining, custodial, transportation, and security services. While Amazon encourages rapid turnover of warehouse staff, employee churn is less desirable for service workers charged with creating a functional and pleasant environment for the company's high-status direct employees and executives. The subcontracted custodial and dining companies also benefit from having experienced workers, so their employees are typically transferred to another campus when the firm loses a campus contract. And unlike the sea of Delivery Service Partners, there are a limited number of large companies able to provide these services at the scale required by a company like Amazon.

Institutional unions have made significant inroads with several campus subcontractors. A national commuter bus firm or institutional food service provider isn't liable to go under after the workers at one location win a raise. These firms have already signed contracts to provide campus services for a set period.[52] And it's a certainty that *someone* will be contracted to provide bus drivers or security for a campus for tens of thousands of workers that cost billions of dollars to construct.

"My assumption is that a lot of these unions are investing in these types of campaigns simply because all these other drives have just not been successful. They've poured in millions of dollars and haven't gotten the results they've expected in terms of dues-paying members," says D, a union organizer in San José.[53]

These positions are still a world apart from those of direct, full-time Amazon staff. Entry-level employees start out making $150,000 a year with health and life insurance, significant stock options, and the promise of unlimited free bananas while at work.[54] And in recent years, it has been workers like these—well-compensated, possessed of formal higher education, and concentrated in relatively stable employment in the urban core—who have proven particularly inclined to organize on the job.

To Organize and Fight

"Every page a victory. Who cooked the feast for the victors?"
—*Bertolt Brecht*

A narrow, syndicalist theory of revolutionary change demands adherence to a blueprint designed to utilize the strategic leverage possessed by manufacturing workers at the point of production in the nineteenth and twentieth centuries.[55] Rejecting this view does not mean forsaking workplace struggle, but it does allow us to appreciate that those waged workers who are most impoverished or precariously employed are increasingly limited in their ability to extract concessions from the fragmented workplaces to which they have been assigned. Those workers most centralized and holding the most strategic power are often gentrifiers for whom the present system works quite well, whose shop floor struggles may express no generalized interest but their own.

There have been widespread successful organizing drives at firms like Starbucks, where small individual work sites are owned by a gigantic conglomerate with a well-known brand and are therefore not subject to some of the same pressures as small businesses.[56] Strikes have also proliferated among graduate students and technical workers—those at least contending for long-term positions at well-off employers.[57]

86

Those employed by small businesses or franchisees, however, have less opportunity to win substantial gains from bosses focused on retaining relatively small profit margins while unconcerned with long-term worker retention. In general, the emergent, spontaneously developing workplace collective action of the precariously employed is not unionization but the permanent walkout, leaving the job not in a strike but a mass resignation. In January 2021, the workers at a Lincoln, Nebraska, Burger King took time to change the marquee's message to "WE ALL QUIT / SORRY FOR THE INCONVENIENCE" before shutting the restaurant down. Eight workers and the general manager resigned after chronic understaffing and weeks without kitchen air conditioning amidst the largest wave of resignations recorded since the Labor Department started keeping count.[58] The description of the Great Resignation as an informal general strike evidently reached such an audience as to inspire a CNBC rebuttal, with Barclays deputy chief US economist Jonathan Miller claiming its "true cause is a hesitation of workers to return to the labor force, due to influences tied to the pandemic such as infection risks, infection-related illness, and a lack of affordable childcare."[59] We should consider that any history of the labor movement that excluded actions related to workplace health and safety or the cost of living (such as childcare) would be both bizarre and rather short.

The historic stability of industrial employment hasn't followed manufacturing jobs, either. The millions of internal migrant workers in China's Shenzhen special economic zone, the "world's factory" that forges 90 percent of the planet's electronics, "might fit the image of an industrial proletariat, but they are treated as a disposable itinerant labour force."[60] These workers lack legal residence permits and access to state benefits including housing and health care, tying them to their jobs until they return home to the countryside. The city has seen mass strikes alongside the most extreme

version of resignation as labor protest: a spate of suicides by workers at massive Foxconn manufacturing plants.[61] As Shenzhen is a
hub for research and design as well as industrial production, rising
housing costs are displacing manufacturing workers farther from
the city's core. Though the city aspires to create 1.7 million affordable housing units by 2035, they will only be available to migrants
with advanced degrees. To make room for these young professionals, 150,000 residents were evicted over the span of two months in
2019.[62] The fact that urban land is supposed to remain the exclusive
property of the state in the Chinese "socialist market economy"
does not reduce the general contemporary incentive for urban displacement in countries connected to the global market.[63]

The tribunes of left-wing orthodoxy contend that to look for
the class struggle beyond the workplace is impossible, as if we shed
our class positions with our uniforms when we clock out at the end
of day. Unions are said to be the "indispensable," "essential vehicle"
for the working class, and struggle that does not narrowly center
them is said to abandon class politics entirely.[64] The crudest, most
objectionable version of this politic declares that those struggling
in the street for Black liberation during the George Floyd Rebellion
were merely deceived—or deceiving—members of what ought to
have been a race-blind, class-reductionist movement.[65] The mouths
open; corpses speak.

"We can accept the collapse of the classical workers movement
and its forms and (continue to) develop and experiment with new
ways to move and analyze," write the authors of "The Interregnum,"
"or we can double down on the impoverished image of past victories and, in our desire, for power, recognition, and leadership,
become the cutting edge of counterrevolution."[66] To look only for
the reappearance of the traditional union form under such conditions risks making it "a means which has gradually been changed
into an end in itself, a precious thing, to which the interests of the

struggles should be subordinated."[67] The revolutionary value of the union-form came from the strategic position of the industrial factory, the potentialities for drawing struggle out from the workplace into the city at large, and the forms of consciousness and life created by the concentration and immiseration of proletarians engaged in shoulder-to-shoulder drudgery. The question that all movements against displacement implicitly contend with is whether "antagonism over access to urban space, infrastructure, and material flows of resources produce a collective consciousness the way that struggles on the shop floor once did."[68]

All the World That's Owned

"when there- /you-are is where-you-were and the sunset groans / into the atlantic, setting blue fire to dark white bones."

—*Evie Shockley*

In 2020, pandemic restrictions encouraged employers to allow workers to perform remote work whenever practicable. Eligible positions were generally more lucrative than those not amenable to a remote transition. Some high-paid workers fled gentrifying cities to continue working for the same salary in cheaper locales. As COVID restrictions waned, companies like Airbnb and Google announced that employees wouldn't be required to return to the office. A sizable number of them took their employers up on the offer and decided to refrain from returning to the epicenters of the "housing crisis." But the gap in wages between polarizing camps of well-off and precarious workers is not a function of certain zip codes. Though corporations and municipal governments often benefit from concentrating certain workers in gentrifying districts, the landlord's incentive to market to the affluent alone does not evaporate outside city limits. "Gentrification is not just something that happened in the inner urban core, and it isn't just big developers, condos, yuppies, etc.," says Nathan Eisenberg of the Bay Area's Tenant and Neighborhood Councils. "Gentrification is the landlord class extracting larger and larger shares of surplus-value via rent."[69]

As professional workers fled gentrifying cities during lockdown, gentrification followed. Through 2020, housing prices shot up dramatically in a slew of small cities and towns across the United States, rising by over 150 percent in Martin, Tennessee (population: 11,500), and more than 50 percent in Kendallville, Indiana (population: 10,000). In the post-post-industrial era, explained one realtor, "the cash flows are better in the Tulsas and Allentowns of the world."[70] The 3,500 largely sexagenarian residents of Port Fairy, Australia, beheld a bewildering transformation, with a developer reporting that by October 2021 fewer than a dozen of the quaint seaside town's homes could be had for less than $1 million.[71]

The concentration of capital, a trained labor pool, and the amenities required to attract them to the urban environment remains advantageous for technology and finance firms for the purposes of recruitment, retention, investment, and labor discipline. The popularity of remote work arrangements does not mean that the tech companies' campuses will fall into the sea or that they intend to retreat from the cities they have sunk millions into. Breathless reports of a 2020 "tech exodus" from the Bay Area were oversold: most of the professionals who left San Francisco just crossed the Bay Bridge to Oakland's Alameda County.[72] A foretold drop in housing costs also failed to materialize. The expected "grand dispersal of tech jobs" turned out to be more of a "modest reshuffling," with large firms generally keen to force employees to return to in-person work in urban tech hubs.[73]

For decades, experts have predicted the imminent death of the physical workplace and the disconnection of geographical location from employment. So far, the tech economy has incentivized the opposite, as employers and educated employees converge in a limited number of "superstar cities."[74] Large, globally connected cities remain one of the key staging grounds for modern capital accumulation, and remote workers are congregating in attractive and connected small cities and towns, not dispersing themselves evenly over the surface of the earth.

But gentrification doesn't spread because of an inherent quality of certain cities. Landlords, banks, and politicians now cater to the highly valorized participants in certain technical industries, a numerically small segment of the population that is so central to profit-making in the contemporary gentrification economy that mass displacement for their benefit proves a lucrative endeavor.

'Midst the Wonders We Have Made

"These super-men and world-mastering demi-gods listened, however, to no low tongues of ours, even when we pointed silently to their feet of clay."

—*W.E.B. Du Bois*

The workers and capitalists who profit most from the gentrification economy are often blessed by familial wealth and almost always with advanced degrees. College-educated workers received a full 97 percent of "good jobs" created after the Great Recession as the labor market polarized between low-paying jobs and those requiring post-secondary education.[75] If it is highly-educated workers who are the crux of production in the wealthy imperial core, and if acquiring such jobs is necessary for workers to achieve not only luxury but a minimally dignified life, it is no wonder that the gentrification economy increases the power and influence of organizations such as the Silicon Valley's largest landowner: not Apple, Amazon, or Google, but Stanford University.[76]

Not only Silicon Valley's largest owner of both commercial land and single-family homes, Stanford University controls a domain including a research park, a shopping mall, a hospital, and professor housing. 61 percent of the university's 8,180 acres are undeveloped entirely, a green oasis of wealth amid a housing crisis.[77]

"People think of Stanford as a university with a football team and two basketball teams, I guess," explains Lenny Seigal, former mayor of neighboring Mountain View. "But it's a corporation with enormous land ownership, and it functions in its relationship to the surrounding communities as a corporation."[78]

And an enormously successful corporation, at that. With a $37.8 billion endowment in 2021, the university has invested billions in income-generating properties.[79] Though it received its land holdings from its founder, robber baron Leland Stanford, the university reaps enormous wealth from a long enmeshment with the tech industry. The relationship dates back to 1937, when two Stanford students founded Hewlett-Packard. Millionaire faculty members invest in students' startups. Venture capitalists teach classes. When graduates—whose median family income is $167,500 to begin with—donate the proceeds of high-paying tech jobs to their alma mater, the endowment grows.[80]

But alumni generosity isn't the only benefit Stanford gets from the industry. The Office of Technology Licensing asserts ownership rights over technology developed at Stanford. Companies like Google, Yahoo, Netflix, VMWare, and Sun Microsystems were all started by Stanford affiliates or using Stanford technology. Cisco's first router was based on the Stanford University computer network. The Office of Technology Licensing received $336 million when it sold its Google stock in 2005.[81] As of 2012, the office had netted Stanford $1.3 billion in royalty payments.[82]

For the privileged children of the Valley, pressure to secure an elite institution's diploma is immense. Parents pad out their children's resumes by dropping thousands of dollars to send them on charitable service trips to Mongolia.[83] Palo Alto paid over a million dollars to install sensors along the commuter rail line to detect attempted suicides when admissions decisions roll in.[84] The city's high school students kill themselves at several times the national rate.

"We are not teenagers. We are lifeless bodies in a system that breeds competition [and] hatred," wrote one Palo Alto High School student in an op-ed entitled "The Sorrows of Young Palo Altans."[85] "If you're not into [science, tech, engineering, and math]," said another, "you feel that you are not going to succeed."[86] The horror that pushes teenagers onto the Caltrain tracks is not of being a worker instead of an owner. It is of falling from the circle of workers who do well in the new economy into those who do not, from those able to gentrify to those only ever displaced.

When universities expand campuses to attract more elite students, they become not only the facilitators and beneficiaries of gentrification, but its agents as well. In Orlando, a $1 billion, sixty-eight-acre mixed-use development around UCF Valencia called the Creative Village caused housing prices to double before construction even began.[87] Wayne State University's private police force enforces security across the gentrified core of post-industrial Detroit. In Philadelphia's so-called University City, historically the Black Bottom, university development has caused housing prices to more than double and the Black population to be cut in half.[88] Universities are now the largest employers in most large cities in the US. "The department store is closed, the newspaper is bankrupt, the local bank is no longer local, and the manufacturing is gone," says Lewis & Clark College president Wim Wiewel. The universities endure, and they have "enthusiastically seized more economic and urban development responsibilities."[89]

And though the right wing claims that colleges are laboratories for the identification of fictitious violence where hoodwinked undergraduates are indoctrinated into believing in the false danger of stereotypes and of slurs, the actual violence of university-facilitated displacement gets scant mention in lecture halls. There are no mandatory freshman courses on the people the new dorm building forced out. Breitbart is not writing outraged screeds about how some mistreated child was "called out" for their techie parents.

Some of the most pernicious and pervasive forms of violence are those not acknowledged as violence at all. Displacement is called rejuvenation, development, revitalization—all biological terms. Such language allows gentrification's proponents to portray themselves as agents of an inevitable natural force, not the instigators of mass dispossession by force, and to react with feigned horror when communal banishment is resisted by force, as well.

All things being equal, people generally find the preservation and self-determination of community and home preferable to the opposite. To convince someone of the futility of such a preference requires an ideological infrastructure of considerable sophistication.

It also requires a certain quantity of loaded guns.

IV. TERROR

"We cannot withdraw from the cities. In order to complete the revolutionary syllogism, the fascists must be forced to withdraw."

—*George Jackson*

One spring day in 2017, the city council of the self-proclaimed "Capital of Silicon Valley" was gathered in a downtown parking lot. Sam Liccardo, former district attorney and then mayor of San José, California, stood in the crisp air behind a podium that staffers had wheeled in for the morning press conference.

The richest city in the United States is not one but two cities, though the working-class Vietnamese and Latinx East Side is just two miles from the $400 million edifice of City Hall. A week and a half before city council's parking lot appearance, a local school district voted to leave three Eastside elementary schools without air conditioning for yet another year, even though, in the words of one teacher, "absolutely boiling" classrooms leave kids "like melted cheese" in the daytime sun.[1] One government report had just counted ten thousand Silicon Valley residents without a home.[2] Another announced that the previous six years had seen 1.5 million Bay Area residents leave in the face of rising rents.[3] And a study released the month before found that you would have to work an average of twenty-four years before being able to put a 20 percent down payment on a San José home.[4]

Any announcement momentous enough to bring local government to an empty lot should be expected to address such distressing realities—though perhaps not in the way that San José's majority of working-class residents would hope. In front of rolling cameras, Mayor Liccardo proclaimed that the city was in negotiations to sell over two hundred acres of public land to Google for a new campus. It would be twice as large as the company's headquarters in Mountain View, and it would bring twenty thousand highly paid tech employees to a city where working-class people were already being forced out. "We will transform this collection of industrial parcels and parking lots," the mayor said, "into a dynamic, vibrant epicenter of technology and creativity."

The mayor's words seemed a little strong. By his telling, there was no question that "the parcels and parking lots" would be "transformed" into a technology epicenter. There was no room in his statement for the possibility that rezoning the area and coordinating the sale of land from multiple public agencies would not be successful. There was certainly no concern that San José residents would oppose a project that would bring tens of thousands of well-compensated tech workers into a gentrifying city. The mayor being flanked by his city council only added to the sense of finality. Though on paper this was the very first public announcement of preliminary discussions for a potential project, the effect was to make Google San José feel like a done deal.

In fact, starting almost four months earlier, seventeen San José city employees began signing non-disclosure agreements with the company, preventing them from publicly discussing negotiations for the next five years. And two months before that, Google purchased the huge Pacific Bell building right next to the proposed site. The inclusion of the public was an afterthought in a bumbling, absurd tragicomedy of managed democracy.

A week after the parking lot press conference, city council began closed-door negotiations with Google. Though California's Brown Act required that such sessions be recorded, the recordings disappeared through an unfortunate technical error. A week after that, the city voted to begin negotiations with Google over the land sale, though Google was evidently confident enough in the negotiation's eventual outcome to have already spent $100 million on downtown land acquisitions.[5] Later that summer, one city staffer opined to another that discussing the project's impacts would be "to [sic] much to give the Council or public at this stage of the process."

In February of 2018, a year after politicians began signing NDAs and eight months after the formal start of negotiations, it was time to drum up some popular support. The grotesque imbalance of power between the finance, real estate, and tech firms that sponsor gentrifying mega-projects and the exploited communities who stand in their way means that the former often see little threat in inviting a degree of public input, though always controlled and contained within official channels. "We look forward to hearing feedback on our proposed development and working closely with the community and city of San José to create a shared vision for a vibrant, mixed-used, transit-oriented destination," said Google's Javier González. A group of "stakeholders" like developers, tech-funded nonprofits, and the company itself began meeting as the Diridon Station Area Advisory Group (SAAG) to "listen to concerns." "The Google project," said the city's director of economic development, "is just a concept," so the SAAG charitably solicited public comment in what local news reported was a "quest to gather and process citizen input."[6] Such citizen input was evidently not needed for the negotiations that Google and the city had at that point been conducting behind closed doors for the greater part of a year.

SAAG meetings were immediately disrupted by outraged community members, who at one meeting held the floor for forty-five minutes chanting "*San José no se vende, ¡Se ama y se defiende!*" until removed by police. San José is not for sale; it's loved and defended. The city took to announcing SAAG meetings with only a day's notice to preempt further disruptions.

"We did direct action because the 'community process' created by Google and the city was not a legitimate process, so we didn't want to participate in that and give it any legitimacy. It was direct action to interrupt and disrupt those places and put out another response which was not, 'We want Google money in San José.' It was like no, we don't want Google, and it was a small group of folks who had the courage to actually say that out loud," says Liz González, one of four co-founders of San José's anti-Google campaign. Another, Katherine Nasol, rejected liberal criticisms of the SAAG meeting disruptions, writing that confining dissent to public channels put up as window-dressing would be to ignore the material reality of Silicon Valley's "local war on the poor." While the advisory committee pondered the tweaks to the project that might improve its "equity," she insisted on community control over land.[7] If struggle against gentrification is to struggle against land as commodity, it must also be a struggle against the government that enforces its commodification. Anti-gentrification movements keep running up against public, private, and nonprofit institutions that preach equity and inclusion while ensuring that the parameters of public debate never stray too far from endorsing projects sure to create mass exclusion through gentrification. The struggle against displacement implies a struggle for autonomy.

The high point of San José city government's buffoonery came that December, when the council was scheduled to sell the city's share of land to Google. For hours, armed police officers looked on as one person after another spoke against the campus, outraged that acres of land would be used for a tech campus instead of afford-able housing. Between these testimonies, the odd developer voiced support for the development, along with non-profit executives who praised the company for their recent strategic financial donations. Groups of protestors, organized as Serve the People San José, rose from their seats to chant "San José is not for sale!" until police escorted each of them from the council chambers.

Finally, a group of eight began chanting and refused to stop. When police tried to pull them from their chairs, they found that all eight had locked themselves to their seats with heavy metal chains. The cops cleared the entire chamber as they waited for someone to bring bolt cutters so they could take the protestors to jail. And then, in an empty hall at two in the morning, with a row of armed police blocking the doors, the council voted unanimously to sell the land to Google.[8]

Forcing Displacement

"show me / an artifact of city which has the power / as flesh
has power, as spirit of man / has power"

—*Diane di Prima*

Gentrification is sometimes talked about as if it were an automatic
process outside of human control, a mysterious, powerful, impersonal force large enough to thwart the best intentions and most
concerted efforts of the politicians and CEOs doing everything in
their power to thwart it. There are always more studies to fund and
interventions to unveil as if economic displacement were a cata-
strophic act of nature, an inevitable force "above politics," which
hapless, well-meaning leaders—including the richest men in
human history—might only respond to as best they can.[9]

   "Google and San Jose hope to make the city more affordable
for working- and middle-class families, but they make matters
worse," reports an article in *The Atlantic*.[10] "My job is to help New
Yorkers live in New York. It's not to clear the place out and see it
fully gentrified," said former Sandinista fellow-traveler Bill de Blasio
while campaigning to be mayor of New York.[11] After the election, he
would restore a program granting tax exemptions to new private
developments for a generation after their construction, so long as a
minority of their units were initially "affordable"—though there was

no prohibition on raising rents immediately thereafter.[12] A granular analysis of the "affordable housing" rezoning of SoHo found "the scheme is structured not only to allow but actually encourage and incentivize construction that contains no affordable housing."[13]

"Go back to Iowa, you go back to Ohio. New York City belongs to the people that were here and made New York City what it is," thundered former police officer Eric Adams to the applause of a largely Black audience before he was elected as de Blasio's successor. Once in office, he would walk back promises to fund affordable housing production while crowing about advancing the "dignity" of unhoused New Yorkers through encampment sweeps.[14]

In 2018, Austin mayor Steve Adler's Anti-Displacement Task Force unveiled recommendations for stopping the "epidemic" of displacement, "the most serious threat we as a city face today."[15] One month later, Adler would appear at a press conference unveiling Apple's plans to build a huge new tech campus within city limits. Despite the task force's suggestions, no affordable housing would be allowed on the fifty acres of open space that would surround the campus as an environmental preserve. "Austin and Apple share a creative spark," said Adler, "a commitment to getting things done."[16]

Rather than an unforeseen catastrophe, gentrification is "very much an economic and social plan where the state collaborates with private investors, capitalists, to exploit areas in a particular city or region where there's 'room to grow,'" in the words of San José's Daniel González.[17] When residents are displaced to fatten capitalists' pockets, the state accompanies them every step of the way.

It is, in the last instance, the state's armed wing, the police, who enforce evictions and stand between empty houses and houseless people. But this is far from the extent of the state's active construction of mass displacement. In the wake of deindustrialization, it was federal "anti-poverty" programs that funded "urban renewal" initiatives against previously underinvested, redlined

Black neighborhoods that had been excluded from New Deal-era government lending programs.[18] Current city tax structures push out longtime working-class homeowners in a country where a family home is the main mechanism for inter-generational wealth transfer: as the assessed value of homes in gentrifying neighborhoods increases, the tax burden on existing residents does, too. Austin municipal property taxes more than doubled from 2006 to 2015. Poor elders were the most likely to miss tax payments as residents were pushed out of desirable neighborhoods.[19] In 1980, Alda Ballard spent $20,000 for a Philadelphia home now worth over $420,000. Philadelphia only offers relief from property taxes for ten years for new or refurbished developments, those generally marketed towards more affluent newcomers. "They are being incentivized to replace us," says a local pharmacist. "They grin and say hi, because they have been promised that we will be gone soon."[20]

And a decade and a half before the Google development was announced, the San José city government declared a third of the land within its borders blighted, allowing properties to be seized and handed off to private companies for redevelopment.[21]

A limited focus on the individual gentrifier as the agent of displacement not only obscures the economic and racial structures that incentivize the process, but also conceals the fact that, as the authors of a study of gentrification in the global South put it, "the key actor in planetary gentrification is the state—neoliberal or authoritarian." Whether yuppies reaping tax abatements for Philadelphia condos or tourists strolling the "cleansed" streets of Sao Paolo, the gentrifier inhabits an environment intentionally constructed by the state to attract her.[22]

"When Google announced plans to move into San José, no everyday person I would talk to wouldn't agree that Google moving in would be devastating for the city," says Vasudha, who organized against the development as a student.[23] But for local state elites, the San José Google development was a fait accompli from the moment it was dreamed up. Turning down a massive tech campus with its accompanying spending power and tax revenue would, for the political class, be unthinkable. The task wasn't to drum up support, much less come to agreement, but to ensure that potential resistance to the plan would be stillborn.

In city after city, local elites choose to approve corporate mega-projects against the interests of their current constituents. The city-as-government plans the economic development of the city-as-territory at the expense of the city-as-community. To appreciate the violence that this linguistic slippage conceals, we might consider that in antiquity, the city and the people were one and the same. The Greek word *polis* referred both to the city and its citizens. To speak of removing the citizens from the city would be a contradiction in terms, an unspeakable act in the most literal sense. To commit such an act against a people because of the prosperity of those who will replace them is an abomination. It is killing the city for the benefit of its owners. A municipality's elected representatives are free to act as the executioners of their constituencies because it is the nature of displacement that many will be replaced with wealthier, whiter constituents before the next election cycle.

"I personally feel like electoral politics is a way of placating people. City councils have donors and they're worried about re-election, so if something's unpopular with donors, even if it's popular with their own community, they're not going to vote on it," says Jenna from Southern California. "There's a lot of structural things in place that make electoral politics really hard to engage in, and a lot of folks in the community can't vote."[24]

Politicians have an incentive to court gentrifying industries regardless of their ideological commitments or community ties. A working-class kid from the projects born to immigrant parents,

Ed Lee became a civil rights lawyer for San Francisco's Asian Law Caucus. He represented two hundred tenants during Chinatown's first rent strike and fought the demolition of working-class housing for redevelopment. Upon taking office as mayor in 2011, he briefly called for a private developer to "substantially fulfill" affordable housing goals as a condition of project approval. By 2015, his administration's proposed "Affordable Housing Density Bonus Program" would have allowed for new market-rate units on tens of thousands of sites across the city: "gentrification on steroids." Lee's signature homelessness policy was bussing the unhoused out of the city. His largest supporter ended up being tech investor Ron Conway. The former champion of tenants' rights oversaw the largest expansion of wealth inequality in the city's history.[25]

In the words of the Affordable Housing Network's Sandy Perry, "We're fighting a huge economic system which is more powerful than any city government."[26] It is not that municipal governments jealously court redevelopment merely because of the moral or political failings of those in power. A city council composed of saints would still find securing a new Google or Apple campus politically irresistible. It would be political suicide to scorn the industry that's the difference between post-industrial Detroit and post-industrial Silicon Valley.

"The city is very pro-development, although a majority of the people sitting on our city council are pretty progressive. The city in general is very heavy on development, including luxury development," reports David Carbajal Torres from Santa Ana. "For the past decade, it has really focused on redeveloping areas in our city that are historically Latinx, historically underserved."[27]

The objective of corporate and state elites is less manufacturing consent among those about to be priced out than to repress any popular resistance that might scare investors and prospective new residents. This is doubly true when the those targeted for removal are oppressed communities already viewed not as constituents but as targets for the racial violence of the capitalist state. When the state's strategic objective is preventing the emergence of oppositional resistance among suspect subject populations, speaking of a lack of democracy, decorum, or due diligence on the part of politicians and bureaucrats misses the point entirely. The governing logic of contemporary urban mass displacement is counterinsurgency.

Peace Machines

"Let the martial songs be written, let the dirges disappear."
—*Margaret Walker*

Counterinsurgency is a doctrine concerned with preventing the emergence of a proto-revolutionary insurgency through both political and military means, particularly focusing on the relationship between the insurgent and the broader civilian population. US counterinsurgency doctrine (COIN) in its modern form is said to date from 1962's National Security Memorandum 182.[28] Five months earlier, the US military in Vietnam had started forcibly "corralling peasants into armed stockades" through the Strategic Hamlet Program, an attempt to rout Viet Cong guerrillas by "draining the sea" of potential popular support.[29] The following years would see hundreds of mass uprisings across US cities as politicians, police, and academics warned of an emerging potentially revolutionary situation. The Kerner Commission, convened in the wake of the Detroit Rebellion, encouraged the domestic application of counterinsurgency practices developed for foreign military occupations: surveillance and repression paired with social programs to win the "hearts and minds" of Black neighborhoods.[30] At the same time, the military dictatorship in Argentina deployed a "counterinsurgency-driven strategy of slum removal" against socialist-sympathizing shantytowns in Buenos Aires. A few years later, Pinochet would likewise attack squatters to restore middle-class rule in Santiago.[31]

A 1981 article attributed to Yulanda Ward controversially cited unpublished documents said to reveal an explicit federal plan for the "spatial deconcentration" of poor people of color from urban areas as a means of social control.[32] Ward, allegedly politically assassinated, never produced those documents. However, it is a matter of record that experts from defense research institutions like the RAND Corporation and military firms like Lockheed were increasingly called upon to address "traffic, poverty, overpopulation, and crime" throughout the 1960s by urban planners, who viewed urban unrest as a problem on the scale of Soviet nuclear warfare.[33] For over half a century, US elites have analyzed urban ungovernability as a problem of the first order.

Counterinsurgency theorist David Galula identifies four courses of action open to the counterinsurgent state or occupying army: direct action against insurgent leaders, indirect action on the social conditions that produce insurgency, infiltration, and reinforcing the political strength of counterinsurgent forces. Galula recommends the last option, building "a political machine at the grass roots in order to isolate the insurgent from the population forever," as it "leaves the least to chance and makes full use of the counterinsurgency's possibilities." Such political isolation, and not merely the physical destruction of the insurgent or her political organizations, constitutes the condition of victory for the state.[34]

A peacetime counterinsurgent political machine, Galula reminds the reader, "is built essentially on patronage."[35] To achieve an enduring victory, the counterinsurgent patronage machine must "take as much wind as possible out of the insurgent's sails" through the provision of limited reforms.[36] In San José, Google donated millions of dollars to liberal nonprofits in the run-up to the December 2018 land sale vote. The nonprofits campaigning against homelessness and displacement funded their programs with money from the very institutions creating them. In 2017, the Google Foundation gave $500,000 to Somos Mayfair to "support families in accessing greater economic opportunities"[37] and earmarked $1 million for California's first "Latino Nonprofit Accelerator."[38] The month before the vote, Google gifted San José's Destination: Home, People Assisting the Homeless, and Downtown Street Team a total of $450,000.[39]

"Almost every nonprofit in the community received funds from Google," says Sandy Perry. "The support was bought and paid for by Google, so the opposition wasn't able to get enough traction to reverse the vote."[40]

After the land sale vote, Google began "embedding" liaisons, including "several women and people of color," to belatedly build community support for the newly approved development. The company also announced a plan to donate $1 billion for new Bay Area homes, which activists and a local real estate consultant saw as transparently "timed in order for the company to spur goodwill with the community and to help its case in acquiring more land."[41] Google also announced the creation of a $155 million "community stabilization fund" to be overseen by friendly nonprofits and paid out over the course of campus construction.[42]

Throughout the legitimation process, much visible "opposition" to the Google development came from Silicon Valley Rising (SVR), a project of the AFL-CIO South Bay Labor Council and its research and community organizing arm, Working Partnerships USA. While SVR raised concerns and rallied protests against the project, they studiously avoided calling for its outright cancellation. The group organized community forums to raise awareness about the project and solicit ideas for ways to "mitigate its impacts," though the question of whether residents supported or opposed the development was never raised.[43] Were it not for a grassroots campaign from an ideologically diverse formation called Serve the People San José, the only questions raised about the tech mega-project would have been about the "community benefits" attached to it, not whether it was to exist at all.[44] "We don't want the tech industry to go anywhere," said Working Partnerships' executive director. "It's a job producer."[45] Working Partnerships would not falter from this position even after producing a report showing the new campus would increase monthly rents by $765.[46]

In fact, it was crucial for both organizations that the project succeed. Both Working Partnerships and Silicon Valley Rising were granted seats on the Station Area Advisory Group of "stakeholders" interested in the Google development, successfully demanding that the company "make a major financial commitment" to nonprofits like themselves.[47]

"They did a lot of the PR dirty work that Google outsourced to them. They were happy to do that because it meant that they could tap into money for the overhead they have. It was really the perfect campaign for them to center themselves as the brokers between the community and Google. On one hand, they said to the community, you're going to be working good jobs that you can access. You'll be working as a janitor but hey, you're going to be paid above minimum wage. And then the narrative they tell Google and a lot of the tech companies is, your investment, your profits are safe here. We'll make sure that the most radical elements of the community are tamped down with minor concessions, so you should be okay to do business here," says D, a local labor organizer.[48]

The gentrifying mega project is framed as a boon for those most likely to be displaced. Grant-funded nonprofits have become increasingly essential to service provision with the gutting of the welfare state. They also provide some of the most visible forms of community organization and resistance, to the point that many trained in programs for "social justice" have trouble imagining collective struggle outside the NGO model. Nonprofits vie with one another for the same corporate and foundation grants. In their absence, organizers are fired, social centers shuttered, food and clothing drives dissolved. In the context of mass displacement, generous grants from the displacers are intentionally structured to trap the recipients, whose organizational hunger for cash grows with the rising cost of living. If a nonprofit turns down a tech grant, it is the community in which they work and not the multinational corporation that suffers. And if they accept, those who are bulldozing and impoverishing a neighborhood get to present themselves as its biggest supporters.

The most reasonable response for a community-oriented nonprofit might be to take the money and run: to accept no-strings-attached grants even from one's adversaries as long as you fight them all the same. Because this position ensures that the first corporate donation will likely be your last, it's a road much less taken. In general, grant-funded organizations appeal to the corporate benefactors who instigate the problems they donate money to address. This philanthropic co-optation induces "a shift from demands for structural reform to more incremental change within the existing political and economic framework"—that is, within the realities of the gentrification economy.[49]

"Google has raised the bar for how the tech sector can be a responsible member of our community," said the South Bay Labor Council's Jean Cohen. "The labor movement and our community partners have worked collaboratively with Google to make sure this project includes the things working people need." Cohen reported that Google was responding positively to requests that the company ensure that its subcontractors remain neutral when labor unions organize the army of food, janitorial, and security workers on the completed campus.[50]

"It's less a rank-and-file thing than it is the big union bosses saying, 'This is good for you.' A Latina señora that's making $16 an hour isn't gonna have time to go to a City Council meeting and say, 'Yeah, I support Google. I support them gentrifying the shit out of the neighborhood I live in,'" continues D. Whether the new campus displaces their existing low-wage members or not, labor unions only benefit from the addition of thousands of new dues-paying members should the project proceed with the correct strings attached. Once an understanding was reached, the mega-project became not only the patron of the community, the culture, and the democratic process itself—it purported to be the benefactor of the working class, as well.

Diversity, Equity, Insurgency

"If it were only a contest of morality and justice, the capitalists would have been kicked out long ago. We all know all this, too. We just don't always absorb the full meaning."

—*J. Sakai*

While the nonprofit funding trap paints the agents of gentrification as its opponents, it costs little for gentrifying corporations and universities to portray themselves as standard-bearers for progressive values, touting their embrace of multiculturalism and their commitment to the abstract representation of the types of people they price out. Some of Google's cafeteria workers are forced to live in the RV camp just beyond the campus, but they prepare food befitting sophisticated citizens of the world: enchiladas and aguas frescas, shaved jicama perched atop char siu, brisket and spam musubi are all to be had, should you elect to not make a reservation at the table-service Indian restaurant.[51] Queer Chicana theorist Gloria Anzaldúa was honored with a Google Doodle on her birthday. After the 2020 uprisings, the overwhelmingly male multinational corporation released a report proclaiming that "it's through collective action that we can make the largest impact on these deep structural issues."[52] Though the "issues" in question were the company's failure to meet its own goals for employee diversification, the message of such language remains clear. Though the implementation of its noble goals faced a few hiccups, Google, we're made to believe, is all for equity and inclusion. Its expansion is the advance of a fundamentally progressive force.

It has even been claimed that not only are gentrification's engineers benevolent, but that gentrification in and of itself is an advance for social justice. The neighborhoods most profitable for redevelopment are generally neighborhoods of color, and those who enter are usually white. Thus an ethnically homogenous neighborhood becomes more diverse, and those who oppose the entry of white professionals are partisans of racial segregation, writes Héctor Tobar in an incredible *New York Times* op-ed entitled "Viva Gentrification!"[53] This argument only holds if you fail to recognize any difference between the "diversification" of a neighborhood of color by white gentrifiers and the desegregation of a white enclave by those previously excluded. For one thing, the former were generally created by the existence of the latter: disinvested non-white neighborhoods were only created because their residents had been banned from white-only areas, not the other way around. Segregation in the United States was the product not of coincidence or mutual animosity but rather of white supremacy. For another thing, white people are generally not priced out of their homes by desegregation. They endorse racial exclusion for the protection of their houses as investments, not just as dwellings. Such logical details seem to be beside the point for the pro-gentrification commentariat crafting a narrative that the displacement of working-class communities of color is, at the very least, complicated. Any negative effects are certainly unintended by the progressive corporations involved, who compose multiculturalist press releases and donate to community initiatives at every turn.

Nonprofit funding has been used as a tool to capture and constrain resistance since the sector's rapid expansion during the Black freedom struggle of the 1960s. In the face of Black popular support for urban rebellion, foundations even bankrolled militant organizations like the Congress of Racial Equality, which advertised its role as being "to prepare people to make a decision on revolution... [and] whether to take land and resources and distribute them."[54] CORE's leader, Roy Innis, would later declare that the Nixon administration was a friend to Black Power.[55] Tens of millions of dollars flowed into Oakland to offset the Black Panther Party's work to make it their revolutionary base.[56]

The Black Power Conference in Newark brought together 1,300 people from 190 organizations just days after the city's 1967 rebellion. Participants, who passed a resolution in favor of armed collective self-defense, would later learn of the conference's 50 corporate sponsors. The following year, it would be funded by the Clairol hair dye corporation, whose president would inform attendees that "Black Power" in truth meant no more than "equity" and "empowerment."[57] The "corporate scheme of ghetto pacification" (as Robert Allen labelled it) was necessary for the neighborhoods that birthed the uprisings of the 1960s to be opened to white investment and residency.[58]

After the dozens of urban revolts of 1967's long, hot summer, the Kerner Commission's landmark admission of white responsibility for Black urban poverty called for jobs, housing, and education. It also contained a little-remembered appendix that called for expanding National Guard riot control training "as rapidly as possible" and recommended high-level planning for "joint operations" between the police, National Guard, and Army in the event of future unrest.[59] The counterinsurgent patronage machine's generosity only extends as far as is required to maintain the governability of a resistant population. In this endeavor, it is always joined by the police.

Silver or Lead

"Fuck the police and their dead homies."
—*Confrontaciones San José*

"The police does work to further gentrification because places that get gentrified seem to be where people of color live. You just push them out, push them out. Nobody cares where these people go, if they go to the streets, if they go to a different city, is they go to a different state. In wealthier, white neighborhoods, people don't get displaced unless it's from a natural disaster," says San José's Liz González. While self-congratulatory press conferences and flashy cash infusions split opposition to displacement, massive investments in policing allow the state to subjugate and pacify potentially profitable neighborhoods, as in the case of Venice in the second chapter. Breonna Taylor was murdered in 2020 by police looking for an alleged drug dealer thought to be one of the "primary roadblocks" to her neighborhood's redevelopment. Earlier that year, a city contractor demolished eight homes on Taylor's street in a three-week period as part of a $200 million municipal initiative. "When the layers are peeled back, the origin of Breonna's home being raided by the police starts with a political need to clear out a street for a multi-million dollar development project," claims a lawsuit filed by her surviving family.[60]

The same year, Walter Wallace was killed by Philadelphia police a mile away from an area recently slated for redevelopment. "It just seems that when white people decide to come back to a certain neighborhood, they want it a certain way," said one retired teacher upon learning of the plan.[61] After Wallace was murdered, his chosen brother told a reporter, "I see that happening around here. White people moving in. I'm not racist, but where are we going to go? Sometimes it feels like they want to kill us all to make room."[62]

In 2008, there were twenty-eight police reports filed for "disturbances" in Seattle's gentrifying Central District. In 2016, there were 116.[63] That was also the year that police started harassing one Harlem resident for playing dominoes with his neighbors on the sidewalk, something they'd done for decades before.[64] The forcible eviction of street vendors served as the opening shots in a "government-led reconquista" of the Lima, Peru city center for the upper classes.[65] A former Atlanta cop reported that his department began the intensive policing of a Section 8 housing complex in a gentrifying neighborhood at the behest of its owners, who hoped to have enough tenants incarcerated that their property could be demolished and redeveloped. "It dawned on me that the entire system, the entire thing, was just a shitty mafia system," he would later recount.[66]

"Not only will you be priced out, but before you're priced out, life will be hell just because of how policed or surveilled the city will be," says Vasudha.[67]

"Philly says all the time, 'We can't afford to house people, the housing is too expensive,'" says Jazmyn Henderson of ACT UP Philly, "but every time we turn around they increase funding to the police."[68] The same dynamic transpires on the other side of the country. "Santa Ana is one of the deadliest police departments in the country, and that goes hand-in-hand with gentrification," says David Carbajal Torres. "Gentrifiers are the eyes and ears of the police state. They call the cops on us. They consider us a nuisance because of who we are."[69]

"The city is the battlefield of the future whether the US military trains for it or not," according to John Spencer of the Modern War Institute at West Point.[70] In the midst of fierce resistance to the razing of Atlanta's South River Forest to build a $90 million "Cop City" urban warfare training facility, a $33 million "tactical scenario village" mimicking a "typical neighborhood block" was added to plans for a police training academy under construction in Chicago.[71] Massive, often deeply unpopular investments in facilities to train militarized law enforcement for urban warfare suggest that a range of political elites agree with the Army's Strategic Studies Group's assessment that "in the next century, the urban environment will be the locus where drivers of instability occur," with "separation and gentrification... radical income disparity, and racial, ethnic and sub cultural separation" creating "delicate tensions, which if allowed to fester, may build over time, mobilize segments of the population, and erupt as triggers of instability."[72]

Sometimes, the co-optative and repressive functions of counterinsurgency are synthesized in the same organization, like Urban Alchemy, a nonprofit tasked with providing "outreach" to unhoused people during the brutal clearing of Echo Park in Los Angeles. Providing outreach and offering services to the inhabitants of the park's dozens of tents might seem a laudable progressive goal, especially since Urban Alchemy's "Community Ambassadors" were often unhoused or formerly unhoused people themselves. In fact, Urban Alchemy strategized extensively with police and provided them on-the-ground data, leading the After Echo Park Lake research collective to dub them "mercenary brokers of displacement."[73] Urban Alchemy workers were instructed to encourage residents to leave by connecting them with nonexistent resources. After the raid, the group supported government PR efforts to "sell the myth that a majority of the park residents received 'housing.'"[74] In actuality, almost none did.[75] Urban Alchemy's outreach received a similarly mixed reception in San Francisco, with one "ambassador" getting shot in the shoulder.[76]

The Snares of the State

"Revolutionary politics, if they are not to be blocked, must be diverted from politics as such."

—*Régis Debray*

"Direct attack means attacking the campus and those in charge of it without detours, for example through state institutions," contends an article about the successful struggle against a Google development in Berlin. "The Google-Campus Berlin can only be prevented if there are widespread attacks against the project."[77]

When tech writer Sarah Slocum went to a San Francisco dive bar wearing a Google Glass headset in 2014, some patrons uninterested in being recorded ripped it off her face (and allegedly stole her purse, for good measure). This action came amid a wave of tech shuttle bus protests, struggles against another "symbol of privilege" in a gentrifying city.[78] Three years later, a luxury townhome in Philadelphia would go up in flames the same night that new upscale housing units in another neighborhood were redecorated with spray paint.[79] "They left us some messages that said that they weren't happy with our gentrification and they weren't happy with us building," a property manager told the press. "They only attacked the Mercedes, the BMWs, the higher end cars. Their message was pretty clear."[80]

The revolutionary tactic is the one that brings revolution closer. At a particular stage of struggle in a specific context, the most "militant" might be least useful.[81] But even in cases when the liquidation of gentrifier property and offensive actions are not yet the order of the day, it must be understood that a real attack is underway. For the engineering of displacement requires a certain balance of power, a containment of opposition, the conquest of territory, an assemblage of investors and bulldozers, eviction notices and shotguns. Counter-insurgent logic is the logic of war, even when charitable donations and campaign promises are deployed in advance of tear gas and bullets.

"There's a war right now. They want to bring the war to the people? We bringing it right back to them!" proclaimed Melvin Hairston of Philadelphia's People's Townhomes.[82] Though not one waged between the robber baron in coattails and the coal-miner in rags, this war is a class war between those who profit from the gentrification economy and those who do not.[83]

Class war, in this sense, does not begin when the poor take up arms. It is not an event that revolutionaries bring about through militancy in deeds, much less words and gestures. It is rather a concrete analysis of the present and historic state of affairs that may be recognized and engaged or disguised and ignored. The oppressed are not called to begin the class war—but rather to see it through.

War, says Clausewitz, "is an act of violence intended to compel our opponent to fulfill our will." To identify a state of war between the owning and oppressed classes is to recognize that it is in the final instance the policeman's gun, the warden's cage, the threat of early graves that create and recreate the capitalist world generation after generation, day after day. From these issue a whole spectrum of coercions and resistances. Global extraction and exploitation demand a certain distribution of shit jobs and corpses; permitted brutalities and unrestricted luxuries; petty privileges and cruelties, large and small. The perspective of war invites us to think of such occurrences as stemming not from the mere absence of justice but rather from a lopsided excess of force. For if Clausewitz is right that war is politics by another means, politics must be "the continuation of war by other means," as well.[84]

V. WAR

"Únanse al baile / De los que sobran / Nadie nos va a echar
de más / Nadie nos quiso ayudar de verdad."
[Join the dance of those left over. Nobody will miss us.
Nobody really wanted to help us.]

—*Los Prisioneros, "El baile de los que sobran"*

"Riots and strikes proliferate, but fail to cohere into anything larger.
The working class has been dismantled. Nothing is left today but
dead generations united in their separation, shambling through the
fire and the dust." This description of the modern Chinese proletariat is no less apt for the workers in the gentrifying cities of the
imperial core. The "old horizon" of industrialization, urbanization,
and capitalist growth "has disappeared in its entirety, while a new
one has yet to (and may never) appear," continues Chuǎng. "This
means our communism differs in fundamental ways from that of
the last century. Nevertheless, like them we are attempting to navigate out from under a series of crushing contingencies."[1]

The gentrification economy is building a "new gilded age" of
drastic income inequality at a scale last seen in the United States
during the Great Depression.[2] A 2021 poll found that a majority
of eighteen- to twenty-four-year-olds and most Black Americans

of all ages hold a negative opinion of capitalism.[3] Socialism is no longer a forbidden topic in US political discourse, but a resurgent anti-capitalism risks fostering a nostalgia for movements long gone. A segment of resurgent socialism—anarchist, democratic socialist, Trotskyist, and Stalinist—seeks to reclaim the glory of the Left by repeating those steps that brought it the greatest historical strength. The collectives, parties, and organizations of this Left judge community fights such as those against gentrification against the measuring stick of received leftist ideologies. Given that it is these fights that are among the most direct confrontations with a new terrain of accumulation and expulsion under contemporary capitalism, we should wonder if it might be more useful to measure our received knowledges against their utility to anti-displacement struggles, instead.

The invigorated politics of economic class has a fraught relationship with the politics of representation and identity. In its coarsest form, the politics of representation threatens to erase the contest for power between the powerful and the oppressed, instead asking the oppressor to recognize the marginalized and ensure that a proportionate share of the elite are plucked from their ranks. Universities and corporations now promote their commitments to "diversity" and "equity," appropriating the language of liberation and revolt while steamrolling the very communities from which they have stolen it. While Juneteenth was added to Google Calendar, Google's workforce is less than 5 percent Black—though their cafeterias are staffed and bathrooms cleaned by a subcontracted Black and brown underclass.[4]

The cynical corporate capture and deployment of identitarian representation has induced some supposed leftists down the road to an unfortunate class-reductionist enclave, claiming that any attention to the realities of race, gender, and sexuality is somehow a counterrevolutionary distraction.[5] This enclave is surrounded by a fantasy world in which the fact that the displaced are disproportionately people of color, and that queer kids and domestic violence survivors unable to afford rent in gentrifying cities are among the first to become unhoused, are somehow frivolous details, irrelevant to the social struggle. Neither liberal representationalism nor class-reductionism have anything to say to the communities facing destruction by the largest agglomerations of wealth in human history.

Presence or Representation

"For I indeed, as absent in body, but present in spirit, have already judged (as though I were present) him who has so done this deed."

—*1 Corinthians 5:3*

Representation is commonly understood through the lens of identity politics, a form of political engagement birthed in part from the communities of what is today the epicenter of displacement. In 1968, students at San Francisco State College, organized as the Third World Liberation Front, began the longest student strike in US history, demanding the creation of a third world college and the reinstatement of English instructor George Mason Murray, a graduate student and the Black Panther Party Minister of Education. After five months of sabotage, mass arrests, and running skirmishes with the police, the school caved by founding the College of Ethnic Studies and with it, Ethnic Studies as an academic discipline.

The strikers framed gaining a foothold in academia as a purely instrumental goal: a means to an end. In the words of one communique: "The Third World Liberation Front and Black Student Union demands stress our human rights to self-determination according to the needs of our community. . . . We must attack from all levels those institutions and persons that have kept us fighting each other and forgetting the real enemy. We must come back to our 'grass roots' understanding that we are all brothers and sisters, and extensions of our communities."[6] Per another: "We urge strikers to reaffirm their commitment to the struggle! Tighten up the picket lines! Fight even harder against racism and for the self-determination of all oppressed people! The people will win!"[7]

In the words of one retrospective, "Black students and the Third World Liberation Front were following revolutions in Africa, Latin America and Asia in leading the strike at what was then San Francisco State College."[8] The purpose of ethnic studies on campus was not to gain institutional recognition, but to prepare communities beyond the campus for revolution. As George Murray himself explained, "We're not just attacked because we're Black Panthers, we're attacked because we're Black people striving to politically educate the masses of the people here in America to create a new system of government that will be beneficial for all persons involved."[9]

To speak of self-determination is no longer in vogue. The key problem for marginalized peoples in today's gentrification economy is no longer power, we are told, but visibility. Our primary strategic objective is to be represented: on screen, in text, in the boardroom. Which raises the question: to what end?

This is not to say that stereotypes are innocuous or that the existence of positive role models is a triviality. The mystery is not why representation matters, but why it is said to matter so much to the exclusion of so much else. The idea of representation has eclipsed the question of liberation for marginalized people in popular discourse, perhaps because it sounds less absurd coming from the mouths of corporate executives or their ad agencies. To speak of representation in a college as a stepping-stone towards building collective resistance is a strategy for liberation. To speak of representation in elite college admissions, Google Doodles, and upper-management positions as self-evident ends is not.

The lingering question is how such representation would materially help the majority of people of color or women or queer people who, we must remember, will never be in such roles. For this is the very nature of representation: that it is not you but someone else who has status. Then, through a metaphysical trick, that person stands in for you: you partake in their status as well, though rarely in a way that pays your rent. You are told of your seat at a table in a board room that you are barred from by armed police.

Sometimes, institutional representation is held as an end in itself. Who, after all, could want to be unrepresented? A slightly more sophisticated tack is to claim that once some members of an oppressed group make it to the top, they can use their power to improve conditions for others, ignoring all of the conditioning, self-deception, and compromises such a social climb entails. One of the clearest expositions of this latter perspective is in former Facebook Chief Operating Officer Sheryl Sandberg's *Lean In*, where she writes, "Women will tear down the external barriers once we achieve leadership roles. We will march into our bosses' offices and demand what we need, including pregnancy parking. . . . We can ignite the revolution by internalizing the revolution."[10]

But upper management gets reserved parking anyway. And a mile from Facebook's campus, pregnant women live in RVs after being priced out of their homes. The marginalized groups supposedly represented by the liberal gentrifying institution are the first to be made absent through the violent displacement it funds. Rather than responding to the elite co-optation of identity politics by ceding the ground entirely and rejecting all politics of identity as inherently elitist and reformist, it can be emphasized that those who make it to the privileged interior of an exclusive hierarchy must be the least representative member of any excluded group to which they belong. For any identity, "the part of the group closest to power and resources," writes Olúfẹ́mi O.

Táíwò, "are typically the part whose interests overlap with the total group's the least."[11]

The wealth of a single gentrifier upturns the lives of many more existing residents, as when an extended family is evicted so their home can be sold to a single tech worker. Though big tech firms dutifully daub their logos in rainbow hues during Pride month, they are never overly concerned with the queer youth and elders scrounging for precarious housing in overheated rental markets.

"Cassie came here from Minnesota because she heard that the Bay Area would be more hospitable. But the best she could do was crash at her cousin's place and work part-time at Goodwill. That was the kind of work she could get as a Black trans woman who didn't have access to large support networks. Her cousin's landlord kicked out their whole apartment. Cassie didn't have anywhere to stay, so she got a Greyhound ticket to Missouri. I genuinely don't know if she's alive today," says Emerald from the South Bay Community Land Trust. "One trans guy's parents were helping him pay rent for an apartment. But when his parents found out he was transitioning, they cut off his rent. He slept on the street; he got mugged. He had to move back in with his parents, and they forced him to detransition."[12]

One response in the face of the corporate-friendly representationalism is to deny the possibility of being made re-present in places where you are not, to point out that it is never a demographic segment or defined community that enters the board room or congressional chambers but specific mortals who are not us. To know that you are categorically prohibited from ascending to such refined spaces because of your race or gender is intolerable. The sheer existence of such elite gilded halls amidst destitution and death in the streets, however, is more offensive still.

An observation: the substitution of representation for power has occurred at the same time that huge segments of the economy have become precarious labor. We know in our deepest hearts we will never become a mogul or go viral or perhaps even have a retirement account, but perhaps we might be represented by those who can. In San José, a councilmember spoke of the irony that anti-gentrification organizers dared critique Google spokesperson Javier González, for, like many of them, he was Latino and from the East Side. Shouldn't he be lauded, the councilmember asked, as a success story? Is his success not the very thing the protestors should want? The sheer audacity: to be given a modicum of token representation and want your community to survive, as well.[13]

"There are a lot of folks who are progressive to a certain extent but can't look beyond their own interests when it comes to gentrification," explains Daniel González of San José.[14] Once representation and inclusion are cleaved from community and power, even the agents of displacement can masquerade as the opposite.

Feeling Burned

"The poor, stupid, free American citizen!"
—*Emma Goldman*

"Almost instantly" after Hillary Clinton lost the 2016 election, new members poured into the Democratic Socialists of America (DSA), a previously minuscule organization whose aging membership had languished "for years in relative obscurity" following a decimation of the ranks during the Reagan years.[15] The group was known mostly for its deceased leader, *The Other America* author Michael Harrington. Harrington spent the sixties denouncing the anti-war movement in the name of socialism, got praised by Ted Kennedy, and served as the DSA's eternal chair until the day he died.[16] After Occupy Wall Street forced the topics of economic inequality and class into US public discourse, the remaining DSA members made an audacious gamble: to concentrate on winning the presidency for Bernie Sanders, a man who served on Vermont's congressional delegation for almost a quarter century before launching a bid that even sympathetic observers counted among "the unlikeliest of prospects."[17]

Though he wouldn't take the Oval Office, the bet paid off. Sanders's unexpectedly strong primary showing pushed "democratic socialism" into the mainstream of US political discourse. To explain what such a thing looks like in practice, DSA leaders cite the example of "Nordic model" Scandinavian social democracies.[18] These Scandinavian social democracies feature a constrained capitalism, where private for-profit companies are joined by extensive public employment, expansive trade unions, and a welfare state pursuing redistributive taxation and spending policies.[19] (Such dubiously-socialist policies in fact closely track those advocated for by President Franklin Delano Roosevelt in his 1944 State of the Union.)[20] Though "joining every other major country on Earth and guaranteeing health care to all people" is certainly a laudable goal, defining Medicare for All as a socialist lodestar sets the horizon of anti-capitalism as the government reimbursement of privately owned hospitals and pharmaceutical companies: the minimal form of the public provision of healthcare common to all other wealthy, (post)imperial nations.[21]

In addition, the gentrification economy presents a far different field of action than that historically navigated by northern European socialists to build the actually existing social democratic states of today. Scandinavian socialism developed alongside urbanization and trade union organization in the 1870s. Tensions between the revolutionary and reformist wings of big tent socialist parties grew with the region's belated industrialization into the First World War and Russian Revolution, an event as offensive to the electoral reformists as it was distressing to the ruling political class. After the pro-Bolshevik socialists split off, the remaining social democrats successfully funneled the "intense class conflict" waged by a mass, militant labor movement into popular votes for welfare state reforms.[22] It was the split from the pro-Bolsheviks, the mass labor unrest of a militant union movement, the pressures of the Great Depression, and fears of impending revolution on the part of the ruling powers that allowed for the social democratic compromise to take hold.[23] The same dynamic prevailed prior to the brief successes of electoral socialism in the early-twentieth-century United States. Before becoming a five-time US Socialist Party presidential candidate, Eugene V. Debs rose to prominence as a labor leader during the bloody Pullman Strike and as co-founder of the Industrial Workers of the World.[24]

The democratic socialist argues for the pragmatic utility of gradualism and the mass appeal of the Nordic model. But Scandinavian social democracy was the rearguard of a revolutionary mass labor movement, an unruly threat grown in factories staffed by a newly urbanized proletariat, a threat so terrifying to economic elites that they were willing to grant significant concessions so long as they were not deposed entirely.

This is far from the prevailing trend in the US—or in modern Nordic nations, which over the last three decades have turned towards free trade, privatization, and anti-immigrant policies. The Heritage Foundation now ranks Denmark, Iceland, and Finland as more capitalist than the US. Sweden cut corporate taxes to become "a leading innovation hub in Europe that's able to attract foreign capital to growing companies." In the neoliberal gentrification economy, a strong welfare state is no longer a winning bet, especially when the Stockholm tech industry can be grown until it ranks behind only Silicon Valley in "tech unicorns per capita."[25] In Denmark, the ruling Social Democrats court Islamophobic voters with plans to raze public housing in immigrant "ghettos," displacing eleven thousand people with the objective of breaking up immigrant communities in order to achieve forced social integration. To ensure the cleansed areas remain attractive to private investors, the party plans to restrict public housing in them afterwards.[26] Meanwhile, the World Bank ranks Denmark as the third best country to do business, with Copenhagen's tech industry "buzzing."[27] As "challenged" by de-industrialization, wage polarization, and population transfers as its American counterpart, the fabled Scandinavian labor movement "continues to justify its existence . . . with reference to their glory days."[28]

"Although the U.S. labor movement is currently in decline, it, too, could come back," George Lakey optimistically explains in the DSA's *Democratic Left*. After all, he reminds us, "Nordic unions also suffered their ups and downs."[29] Half-remembering that the election of socialist politicians was only ever the rear-guard of advancing militant labor movements, democratic socialists cling on to any labor action at hand: a unionized brewery in San Francisco; a (debatably) wildcat strike by West Virginia teachers, a brave and inspiring action almost sure to not stop the gutting of public education.[30] But growth from an emergent mass labor movement is a qualitatively different dynamic than recruiting based on ideals articulated in an electoral campaign while waiting for a non-bureaucratized, militant movement to magically appear. The historic success of one does not imply the feasibility of the other, especially when the "left wing of the possible" creeps rightwards in the countries with the strongest democratic socialist traditions.[31]

What Was to be Done

"New territory. A thousand problems. Only experience is
capable of correcting and opening new ways."
—*Rosa Luxemburg*

The major state socialist alternative to electoral reformism has
historically been vanguardist Marxism of various varieties:
Marxism-Leninism, Trotskyism, Maoism, and Third Worldism. The
Party for Socialism and Liberation (PSL) grew dramatically during
the Trump administration, rushing to call for demonstrations
around hot-button issues and build name recognition with a bot-
tomless supply of branded picket signs. Though descending from a
Trotskyist tradition that matched the defense of the Soviet "workers'
state" with a call for an additional political revolution against its
ruling Stalinist "bureaucratic clique," the PSL offers full-throated
support of a smorgasbord of one-party states based on the theory
that class struggle is primarily the conflict between capitalist and
socialist "camps" of nation-states.[32]

The great irony is that "campism" achieved real prominence in
the United States only after the USSR's evaporation and China's
market reforms: that is, after the decisive implosion of the "socialist camp." Uber and Lyft grew as two beneficiaries of the billions
of Chinese yuan invested in US tech firms—$18.7 billion in 2016

alone, before Trump administration restrictions.[33] One top-rated "Global Executive" MBA program takes students between modules in Silicon Valley and Shanghai, together with the fellow gentrifying global cities of London, Paris, and New York.[34]

Despite recent restrictions on Chinese imports and investment, the US and Chinese national economies remain profoundly linked. The United States justified a campaign against Chinese tech firm Huawei as a principled defense of the rule of law and national security. Campists saw the move as part of an imperialist plot to overthrow Chinese socialism.[35] What both narratives leave out is the competition between the US and Chinese governments over which nation's tech sector will set global standards and assure its citizens privileged spots in the gentrification economy. Behind the discourse of rights and rules lies the struggle for "global dominance of the payment system," "technological superiority," and the efforts of both states to maintain exclusive control of "technologies for surveillance, facial recognition, and genetic analysis."[36]

Some firms manage to sell guns to both sides of the tech war. Oracle's Endeca Information Discovery, originally developed with funding from CIA venture capital firm In-Q-Tel, was used by Chicago police to identify march routes and meeting places during the city's 2012 anti-NATO protests. Oracle would trumpet this as a successful use case to market the software to the Chinese government, who would join the Defense Intelligence Agency, US Cyber Command, and the FBI as Endeca users.[37]

The Party for Socialism and Liberation assumes the form of a Leninist vanguard party: a hierarchical, closed organization of disciplined cadre, bound by the democratic centralist principal of "freedom of discussion, unity of action."[38] The Leninist party form is heralded by state socialists the world over as the only possible vehicle for revolution, its unilateral governance in a "dictatorship of the proletariat" the only possible mechanism for progressing to the abolition of economic exploitation and the state itself. "In reality," says Errico Malatesta, "one sees a dictatorship of party, or rather of the heads of a party."[39] Leninists dismiss such observations as the work of utopian idealists, pointing to the vanguard party's seizure of state power as evidence that the form corresponds to objective material conditions.

In fact, the democratic centralist vanguard party was initially promoted not as the universal revolutionary form but instead the form appropriate to the exceptional conditions of pre-revolutionary Russia: the severe repression of any socialist activity whatsoever by the secret police, a wave of spontaneous strikes by newly urbanized proletarians unconnected to any political party or formal trade union, the rule of a hereditary autocracy instead of the parliaments of Western Europe.[40] First described as a strategic necessity imposed by Russia's extraordinary circumstances, democratic centralism only gained the stature of a general model after the USSR and China spent decades exporting it, preferring client states with organizational forms easily integrated with their own.[41]

Struggles against mass displacement are among the most acute class conflicts in the contemporary economy. These fights, according to either the democratic socialist or Leninist models of change, are at best useful accessories to the real work, opportunities for fair-weather solidarity and potential recruitment. Concrete conditions suggest a critique of both models of state socialism on their own terms: pragmatic democratic socialism now appears less than practicable, while hard-headed Marxism-Leninism lingers on as an ideological fetish divorced from material realities.

Both ideologies trace their ancestry back to tendencies built, fundamentally, to ensure working-class benefits from the process of industrial expansion, either in the West or in the colonies—the exact opposite of the pattern visible in the contemporary United

States. Many of those who deny this signal their fidelity to plans borne in a bygone world with the unknowingly ironic label "materialist."

Beyond the State, the Metropolis

"This community is the one called the city, the community that is political."

—*Aristotle*

The resurgence of state socialism also ironically coincides with the historic weakening of the nation-state. The yearning for the expansive welfare provisions of bygone governments, like the nationalist frenzy for imposing but ineffective border walls, can be seen as a psychological reflex against the "contested and eroding state sovereignty" of globalized capitalism.[42] Within the neoliberal world market, it is increasingly the individual "global city" that competes directly for labor and capital above and beyond the nation-state that claims it.

Modern cities, writes Jodi Dean, "relate to Apple, Amazon, Microsoft, Facebook, and Google/Alphabet as if these corporations were themselves sovereign states—negotiations with, trying to attract, and cooperating with them on their terms."[43] New York City has its own Department of State, sets its own foreign policy, and has a GDP larger than South Korea or Australia.[44] The World Bank projects that "today's big challenges," from climate change to economic development, "will all need to be met through the responses of cities,"[45] which now are responsible for 80 percent of

global GDP. The wealthiest twenty megacities are home to the lion's share of large corporations. These global hubs are "denationalized" to the point that they "belong as much to global networks as to their country of political geography,"[46] operating as "autonomous global actors . . . poised to seize even greater power in the coming decade."[47] Politics is now, in large part, "a league of traders and city governments acting on a world scale, whose main concern will be to promote the competitiveness of the global firms that they accommodate."[48] But even rich cities are dwarfed by the power and wealth of the multinationals they fight to attract, giving corporations incredible leverage to "ensure they have a global operational space that suits their interests."[49] In such cities, the wealth of the elite sits next to dispossessed peoples drawn from across the world whose communities are now threatened with obliteration. "In the global city, they become present to power and to each other," writes Saskia Sassen. "Thus, these cities are strategic for both global corporate capital and the powerless."[50]

In a 1970 speech at Boston College, Black Panther Party co-founder and Minister of Defense Huey P. Newton announced the abandonment of revolutionary nationalism as the party's political ideology. To aspire for economic, cultural, and political self-determination of the Black nation in the United States was futile, he informed the audience, since capitalist globalization negates national self-determination in general, extracting the wealth of communities across a globally integrated market: a "reactionary intercommunalism" that "laid siege" upon both San Francisco and Hong Kong, both Harlem and Durban. To transfer the wealth and technology of empire to the peoples of the world would require a revolutionary intercommunalism between the oppressed, those not fortunate enough to join an emergent ruling class of technocrats "too specialized to be identified as . . . proletarian."[51] Almost half a century later, a militant from the public transportation uprising in Santiago, Chile, would write to a comrade in Paris: "The crisis of governmentality is general: metropolises of the world, gather together."[52]

Winning the urban struggle is imperative during what has been called an Age of Cities.[53] As the "key node" for the "global flows" of capital, labor, and commodities, reports consulting firm McKinsey, the global city must create "vibrant, livable environments that draw high-caliber talent."[54] To compete in an international "war for talent," urban areas must have enough educated workers to attract global corporate investment.[55] As "smart people are the most mobile," the metropolis must attract them. The concentration of wealth in cities draws people in, while transformation for the benefit of high-paid "talent" requires that more people are pushed out. Gentrification is not only intended: for city elites, it is crucial. "We need more Google cities," lamented Carlo Ratti for the World Economic Forum after Google Toronto's defeat. "More Linux cities, more cities remade by start-ups that no one has heard of yet."[56]

"Our great advantage in the metropolis is that the wealth stolen from us is where we are, on the spot, to demand back," writes Selma James. "For those in the Third World, it is infinitely more difficult to demand the return of the wealth our combined labor has created," she continues. "For most of us the dilemma is that the wealth is not where we are. This poses enormous problems of organization and mobilization of power. Yet we have no choice."[57] The expulsion of the poor from the cities of the rich means those in the imperial metropolis must now confront the same problem.

The Exploded City

"There is no need to fear or hope, but only to look for new weapons."

—*Gilles Deleuze*

The urban core is a well-known site of rebellion and rupture. So too is the impoverished countryside. Both terrains are commemorated and theorized as such, the preferences for specific tactics and strategies appropriate to one or the other serving as the basis for entire ideologies, organizations, and projects of life: the factory strike and plaza occupation, the rural commune and Indigenous autonomous zone, the choice of city streets or rural expanses determining the contours of voter drives or clandestine attacks.

The centripetal attraction of the global city's wealth and the centrifugal repulsion of its accompanying costs push the poor into a third space: the suburbs, exurbs, or ring cities that surround it. These areas lack the population density and services of the main city but are connected to it by infrastructure sufficient to transfer goods and labor throughout the greater metropolitan area. The very heart of a wealthy city still holds great symbolic power as a site of protest, but today, it has often been converted into a daytime shopping district for office workers or tourists. By the time of an evening protest, many low-wage, daytime workers have begun the long commute home, leaving only sterile buildings and armed police as witnesses. This present reality is held down by the weight of historical narrative and myth: the city as the home of urban rebellion, the suburb as a bland sea of middle-class white conformity. We are left with the "ironic phenomenon where a bunch of leftists living in the already-gentrified urban core treated that area like it should be the focus of all organizing and seemed to be pretending that the last decade or two of displacement just hadn't happened," says Phil Neel. The impoverished racialized suburbs, small cities, and working-class neighborhoods surrounding major cities have already emerged as key locations of revolt, from the banlieus around Paris in 2005 to Kenosha and Brooklyn Center in the 2020 uprisings in the United States. "At the same time, there wasn't even an attempt to really think about how you might conduct political organizing in hyper-diverse suburban neighborhoods like that."[58]

"It's essential to be able to fight these battles. We also need to spread them: not just in these high-tech cities where they're displacing people but in the areas where the people who have been displaced have gone," says Sandy Perry.[59]

"When people are scattered, you can't collectively build together in resistance because a lot of action is immediate," says Dezmond of Seattle's Black Frontline Movement. "It diminishes the capacity for people to actually resist the gentrification and the violence that's happening, so it just helps it continue further."[60] To the degree that this dynamic prevails, it is cause not for resignation but reassessment, not for an abandonment of the struggle for thriving and militant joy but an openness to new paths to attain it. "Since in the past we have lost when we didn't ask enough," writes Selma James, "we cannot do worse by demanding everything."[61]

"We're starting to look more like European cities, like Lyon and Paris, where poverty is being pushed into the ring of neighborhoods surrounding cities," says American University's Derek

Hyra.[62] Wealth surrounded by deprivation, the objective terrain of strategic encirclement, is also the pattern of great cities throughout the Americas. Numerous movements around the world have grappled with the same problem confronting us today: how to find focal points to concentrate resistance in the face of expulsion and dispersal. Though some fighting gentrification have strategically engaged with the public processes offered by the state to expose their bankruptcy, none have found that subordinating the collective will for survival to liberal pacifism, "democratic" procedures, or token representation to be sufficient to disrupt displacement.

The Fourth Critique

"But here we are faced with the need to create organizational structures that are capable of regrouping the excluded in such a way as to begin the attack on repression."

—Alfredo Bonanno

In a fragment by Jorge Luis Borges, successive generations of cartographers create increasingly exacting maps of China. Their maps grow steadily larger to incorporate more and more minute details until "the Cartographers Guilds struck a Map of the Empire whose size was that of the Empire, and which coincided point for point with it," for the only map that could communicate every detail of China would be a map on the scale of the country itself.[63] Today, the Chinese maps are even larger than the empire.

The commanding heights of the gentrification economy are tech and biotech firms that collect, systematize, privatize, and commodify inputs such as genetic data, personal information, and behavioral profiles at levels far beyond that accessible through first-person experience: the stuff of ever-growing maps, new material for market exchange. The more perfect these maps, whether of a user's consumer proclivities or genome, the more profits may be wrung. These inputs are not initially purchased from another party. Instead, as Shoshana Zuboff explains, "Surveillance capitalism unilaterally claims human experience as free raw material for translation into behavioral data."[64]

For Marx, capitalism is necessarily based in primitive accumulation, the "conquest, enslavement, robbery, murder, in short, force" necessary for one class to acquire capital and for another to be dispossessed to the degree that it must sell its labor to survive.[65] Marx placed this initial violent accumulation in the late-fifteenth and sixteenth centuries, when English peasants were forced off feudal lands and Indigenous American and African peoples were enslaved.[66]

Peter Kropotkin was quick to critique Marx's "erroneous division between the primary accumulation of capital and its present-day formation."[67] Later Marxists likewise found that primitive accumulation was not a bounded historical event but an ongoing process. Silvia Federici cites World Bank structural adjustment programs that, under the guise of making poor countries "competitive," uproot the "last vestiges of communal property and community relations" and "force more and more people into wage labor," as one example, and the exploitation of women's unpaid domestic labor another.[68] The social, biological, and psychological data now closed off and privatized by capital are a new frontier of such accumulation.

The material limit of appropriation of land is the amount of existing acreage, just as the material limit of the appropriation of iron ore is the quantity found in a certain mine. The gentrification economy is based on the modeling and mapping of the world; its material limit is the representation of the world down to the atomic level. So long as this endeavor remains profitable and requires a small caste of educated technicians, the gentrification economy and the struggles against displacement may only be expected to continue.

There are at least three lines of popular political critique of the tech economy aside from resistance to community displacement. One critique of tech companies concerns their management of platforms that serve as a semi-public space. The prohibition or promotion of certain content or communities is criticized from the perspective of users. There is also a line of critique from the perspective of those subjected to new forms of power: quantified, mapped, and modeled. And warehouse workers, rideshare drivers, and software engineers alike criticize their tech industry employers from the perspective of workers. The struggle against gentrification is a critique of a fourth type. In addition to the user, the subject, and the worker, there is the resident. The Block Sidewalk campaign in Toronto joined an anti-gentrification fight to people's concerns about surveillance technology and US corporate encroachment: resistance on the terms of the subject as well as that of the resident. The fight to kill Amazon's New York campus highlighted both how housing costs would rise and how few local residents would get high-paying jobs: the resident and worker. The fight against Google Berlin pulled together opposition "from the displacement of the neighborhood, through data abuse of Google, to criticism of power and technology," the synthesis of such critiques "made possible by a shared intensification of a social conflict."[69]

From the perspective of the ruling class, existing residents are residual, remainders, leftovers. "Join the dance of those left over," goes Los Prisioneros' song, an anthem of the movement against Pinochet that found new life during Chile's 2019 Estallido Social.[70] "The games ended for others with laurels and futures. They left my friends kicking stones."[71]

It is hard to imagine a demand more modest than the maintenance of one's home, community, and life. And yet to stop displacement would demand, as Vasudha puts it, "a reimagining of the current socio-economic system, because as it currently exists, gentrification is incentivized and encouraged until every cent of profit is milked out. The last 200 years of housing policy and how the 'market' works is encouraging and incentivizing gentrification. To stop it will require masses of people to really come together and pitch in and make sacrifices to a larger movement to restructure the socio-economic system as it currently exists." The reasonable demand for universal housing in an economic system based on private landownership is a "non-reformist reform" in the original sense outlined by André Gorz: not an especially progressive reform to demand of the capitalist state, as the democratic socialists would have it, but an apparent reform that in fact could only be instituted by a "fundamental political and economic change" created through the "autonomous power" of the dispossessed.[72]

We must unfortunately still contend with those whose superficial concern for the oppressed is outweighed by a greater fear of the oppressed developing just such an autonomous power. Neither the benevolence of corporate charity nor the "proper channels" offered by local representative democracy have proven, in any city in the world, sufficient to halt economic gentrification. Yet the partisans of propriety and moralists of reform continue to insist that those facing displacement and death restrict themselves to permissible tactics proven to fail. And so homes continue to be destroyed and our neighbors continue to expire on the streets. The hands of the self-declared pacifists drip with blood as their throats fill with empty platitudes. Those who demand decorum and reasonableness in resistance are accessories to the most indefensible outrages.

"I don't know that we can challenge gentrification on political terms," says Daniel González of San José. "It's going to require a lot of militancy. Not just militancy, because you need a multi-faceted approach to enable greater participation. But you do need to have a very real and material threat to the stakeholders, to the city, to the investors. It needs to go beyond the arena of representative politics."

A New Civilization

"aunque ya no tengamos para cuándo volver / pero con la certeza de que toda realidad siempre será más rica / que el mapa incomprensible de nuestra propia nostalgia."
[Though we no longer have a date to go back, but with the certainty that all of reality will always be richer than the incomprehensible map of our own nostalgia.]

—*Mario Payeras*

Margaret Thatcher, Hewlett-Packard's David Packard, George H.W. Bush, and Mikhail Gorbachev walked into San Francisco's Fairmont Hotel on a clear autumn day in 1995. NATO had just suspended airstrikes in Bosnia, eBay was barely over three weeks old, and Mariah Carey's "Fantasy" was still atop the charts as five hundred of the world's leading politicians, executives, and academics arrived to the State of the World Forum. The conference's mission was for this "global brains trust" to sketch the "new civilization" to come after the dawn of the millennium. Over its duration, a consensus would form among participants that the key to the security of this emergent order might be summed up in a single word: *tittytainment*.[73]

Tittytainment, explained former National Security Advisor Zbigniew Brzezinski, would be necessary to satiate and pacify the 80 percent of the population rendered inconsequential to the global economy by the changes to come. "The bottom eighty per cent will have almighty problems," declared economist Jeremy Rifkin. The choice will be "to have or be lunch," in the words of Sun

Microsystems's Scott McNealy. Physicist Rustum Roy suggested that what is now commonly referred to as universal basic income might prove useful, in conjunction with Brzezinski's anesthetic tittytainment, in placating the superfluous masses. "A new social order is being sketched out at the Fairmont—one of rich countries with no middle class worth mentioning—and nobody there disagrees," reported one of the few journalists in attendance. "In any event, the business leaders expect that, soon, in the industrialized countries people will again be sweeping the streets for next to nothing or find a meagre shelter as household helps."[74]

The 20:80 society sketched out in 1995 would prove a self-fulfilling prophecy.

A generation later, twenty-five hundred Twitter employees would work out of the massive Western Furniture Exchange building a dozen blocks to the south of the Fairmont Hotel. Hundreds would live and die on the streets of the Tenderloin neighborhood in between, squeezed between soaring rents, fentanyl-laced overdoses, and the cops unleashed by a tough-on-crime "state of emergency" declared by the Democratic mayor.[75]

A 2016 World Bank report called wealth polarization "perhaps the biggest risk from technological change," with the tech economy's benefits "most likely to be captured by those already better off."[76] "With gentrification and an influx of wealthier residents, housing is out of reach for some families," lamented the DC Chamber of Commerce two years later.[77] A year after that, the International Monetary Fund's Finance & Development magazine would award first place in an essay contest to an article discussing climate gentrification in Miami.[78] The World Economic Forum promoted community land trusts as a "solution to the global housing crisis."[79]

None of this means that arch-capitalist institutions oppose the gentrification economy gold rush. But the social tensions it stokes have the potential to become so great that they threaten to outpace the benefits such an economy provides to its owners.[80] It is because they recognize the powder-keg within the gentrifying city that elites are so desperately working to dampen the fuse.

Notes on Practice

"& tonight, when we dream, we dream of dancing / in a city
slowly becoming ash."

—*Danez Smith*

Within these conditions, to demand fidelity to the historical
forms of anarchisms past would be as inappropriate as democratic
socialist or Leninist historical reenactment. The lineage of political anarchism traces back to the same industrial conflicts and
same mass workers' movements that birthed state socialism. In
the aftermath of the Lyons workers insurrections of the 1830s, the
first self-described anarchist, Pierre-Joseph Proudhon, declared
that the socialist struggle began in the "war of the workshop,"
with the workshop "the building block of the new society."[81] But
it was not until the International Workingmen's Association (First
International) was founded, in 1864, that anarchism became a
movement. Just seven years later, "the political orientation of the
majority of the internationalists in Italy, Spain, and the Swiss Jura
was anarcho-syndicalist in all but name."[82] The Industrial Workers
of the World counted 150,000 members in 1917.[83]

In the United States, "anarchism as an organized movement virtually disappeared after the depression. Before the Second World
War, Emma Goldman returned to the United States, agitated on

behalf of her Spanish comrades, but was taken up more as a relic of a bygone era than as an exponent of a dangerous creed."[84] Little wonder that the anarchist orthodoxies forged during this period might ring more than a little hollow today. This is doubly true when we consider the characteristics of some of the most emphatic keepers of the faith. The social base of anarchism is transformed not only quantitatively but also qualitatively, with the smaller milieus of today not often rooted in communities of immigrant laborers, as was the IWW of yore, but frequently tied to predominantly white punk scenes. A continuity of slogans does not imply a correspondence in the possibilities of struggle. Reminiscing about the anarchist Barcelona of the 1930s provides no clearer guide to struggle in the post-industrial city than hallucinations of Bolsheviki atop the steps of the Winter Palace.

"Our left subculture," writes J. Sakai, "uses the Russian Revolution of 1917 and the conflicting stalinist and anarchist experiences of the 1937 Spanish Civil War as its framework. So discussions on a key subject are familiarly conducted at a remove—using the puppetry of actors and scenarios from almost a century ago, on a different continent; none of it in our living memory or knowledge." Sakai correctly points out that many of Marx and Bakunin's specific interventions are for all intents and purposes "untranslatable," such is the "complex barrier that divides our reality."[85]

But if navigating pro-gentrification counter-insurgent schemes requires movement beyond political representation, severe suspicion of state power, and radical insistence on the self-determination of the oppressed, we might describe those engaged in such maneuvers as already having adopted an anarchism of praxis. This practical anarchism would not see itself reflected in the doctrinaire anarchism(s) of ideologists and subcultural norms. Its protagonists might describe their beliefs in any number of ways. It would grow out of, not be extended to, the "inherently anarchistic element" of those who are displaced first: the Black, Indigenous, and immigrant communities already "residents in" and not "citizens of" the United States.[86] The anarchism of praxis is the practice of survival for those targeted for removal by capital and the state.

In the gentrifying cities of the world, encampments and block-ades, occupations and sabotage, parties and street art, clandestine subterfuges and riotous acts are some of the nuclei of struggles against mass dispersion, racial terror, and communal obliteration. There are surely forms of struggle yet to come that we have not yet discovered, future convulsions that might not be so legible to those only looking towards the past, given the seismic shifts in produc-tion and urban composition that have transpired. Each community has its own trajectory of resistance and loss. Each city has its own architecture of lived practice and collective sense. All are fighting to construct a base and ensure a home on shifting terrain. Their actions are focal points to concentrate resistance against the cen-trifugal force of dispersal.

"We're so used to being marginalized. It would be really great for our anti-displacement work if our elders could interact with folks in the community, if their senior housing costs didn't increase past their fixed incomes. We could learn from that elder knowledge and they could acquire chosen family if they didn't have it. Maybe housing shouldn't be tied to your job," says Emerald. "We don't have a way to do that under our current system without the end of capitalism. But we have to start trying."[87]

The rulers pile their gold next to the tent encampments in cit-ies ringed by the displaced. These include key metropolises of the richest and most heavily armed country in the history of the world. The heirs of radical traditions from across the world find themselves assembled together to serve the rich who would then displace them once again. Perhaps the defensive struggles against displacement today can be oriented—organizationally, ideologically, socially—so as to facilitate an eventual pivot towards an offensive politics of anti-gentrification, a struggle whose contours remain to be defined. Survival is but the minimum program; the beast has shown us its throat.

Acknowledgments

Credit for this text must first go to those in struggle. I am especially grateful for the participants in the fight against the Google mega-campus in San José, who allowed me to make small contributions to an immense struggle over the course of several years. I owe a deep debt to all those who spoke to me about their work against the violence of gentrification for this and other outlets: David Carbajal Torres, D, Emerald, Ms. Darlene Foreman, Dezmond Goff, Daniel González, Liz González, Lisa "Tiny" Gray-García, Jazmyn Henderson, Jenna, Bryan Peraza, Sandy Perry, Noni Session, Ms. Jataun Valentine, and Vasudha.

This manuscript benefited from the deep editorial engagement of Kristian Williams and would not have been possible without the work of the Institute for Anarchist Studies and AK Press. Ximena Hernández Goldberg provided invaluable research on Barcelona, Havana, and Mexico City. Clover Hines graciously offered feedback on an early draft.

I would like to thank my partner, Sharoon Negrete González, for their endless support through the protracted struggle of manuscript production and for their encouragement of my writing, which would have remained a vague aspiration without the assistance of them and many others.

Notes

INTRODUCTION

1. "Squatters Occupy Series of Berlin Buildings," *Deutsche Welle*, May 21, 2018, https://www.dw.com/en/berlin-squatters-take-over-series-of-buildings -to-protest-gentrification/a-43864221.

2. George Avalos, "Amid Loud Protests, Google Village in Downtown San Jose Gets a Public Airing," *The Mercury News*, May 23, 2018, https://www.mercury news.com/2018/05/23/google-village-downtown-san-jose-gets-a-public -airing.

3. Charlotte Silver and Abraham Rodriguez, "SF Protesters Say No to 'Techsploitation,' Block Buses with Scooters," *Mission Local*, May 31, 2018, https://missionlocal.org/2018/05/protesters-say-no-to-techsploitation -block-buses-with-scooters.

4. Ebonee Johnson, "Philly Activists Celebrated May Day with a 'Death by Incarceration' Protest," *Generocity*, May 2, 2018, https://generocity.org/philly /2018/05/02/activists-may-day-philadelphia-criminal-justice-immigration.

5. Inga Saffron, "Why the N. Philly Grandmothers Who Shut Down Temple's Football Stadium Meeting Are So Angry," *The Philadelphia Inquirer*, March 8, 2018, https://www.inquirer.com/philly/columnists/inga_saffron/temple -university-football-stadium-stompers-north-philadelphia-20180308.html.

6. Gillian McGoldrick, "Analysis: Who Are the Stadium Stompers?," *The Temple News*, October 17, 2017, https://temple-news.com/analysis-stadium -stompers.

7. Sarah Ravani, "$10,000 Reward Offered for Info on Bay Area Tech-Bus Shootings," *SFGate*, February 28, 2018, https://www.sfgate.com/bayarea/ article/10K-reward-offered-for-info-on-Bay-Area-tech-bus-12716356.php.

8. Jennifer Remenchik, "Demonstrators Splash Red Paint inside LA Gallery in Apparent Protest of Gentrification," *Hyperallergic*, April 20, 2018, https://hyperallergic.com/439208/anti-gentrification-protest -red-paint-dalton-warehouse-los-angeles.

9. Alex Crichton, "Protestors Say Hotel Cadillac Symbolic of Gentrification Issue in the City," *WXXI News*, June 8, 2018, https://www.wxxinews.org/government/2018-06-08/protestors-say-hotel-cadillac-symbolic-of-gentrification-issue-in-the-city.

10. Stephanie Golden, "Hotel Cadillac Set to Re-open in 2020," *Rochester First*, June 13, 2019, https://www.rochesterfirst.com/news/local-news/hotel-cadillac-set-to-re-open-in-2020/.

11. Alexander Durie, "The Berlin Neighbourhood Fighting Off the Google Giant: Kreuzberg's Crusade," *Huck*, June 29, 2018, https://www.huckmag.com/perspectives/reportage-2/berlin-neighbourhood-fighting-google-giant.

12. Maev Kennedy, "Chronicler of London Gentrification Priced Out of Shoreditch," *The Guardian*, June 28, 2018, https://www.theguardian.com/uk-news/2018/jun/28/artist-adam-dant-chronicles-london-gentrification-priced-out-shoreditch.

13. Jenna Wang, "Residents Sue Washington, D.C. for Racist Gentrification Practices," *Forbes*, June 28, 2018, https://www.forbes.com/sites/jennawang/2018/06/28/residents-sue-washington-d-c-over-1-billion-for-racist-gentrification-practices.

14. Ruth Glass, *London: Aspects of Change* (London: MacGibbon & Kee, 1964).

15. Loretta Lees, Hyun Bang Shin, and Ernesto López-Morales, *Planetary Gentrification* (Cambridge: Policy Press, 2016), 32.

16. Brenden Beck, "The Role of Police in Gentrification," *The Appeal*, August 4, 2020, https://theappeal.org/the-role-of-police-igentrification-breonna-taylor.

17. Lance Freeman, *There Goes the 'Hood* (Philadelphia: Temple University Press, 2006), 1–2.

18. Daniel González, in discussion with the author, September 2020.

19. Tracy Rosenthal, "101 Notes on the LA Tenants Union," *Commune*, July 19, 2019, https://communemag.com/101-notes-on-the-la-tenants-union.

20. Federal Housing Administration, *Underwriting Manual: Underwriting and Valuation Procedure Under Title II of the National Housing Act* (Washington, DC, 1938).

21. Lee Lacy, "Dwight D. Eisenhower and the Birth of the Interstate Highway System," *Army Sustainment*, February 20, 2018, https://www.army.mil/article/198095/dwight_d_eisenhower_and_the_birth_of_the_interstate_highway_system; Candice Norwood, "How Infrastructure Has Historically Promoted Inequality," *PBS NewsHour*, April 23, 2021, https://www.pbs.org/newshour/politics/how-infrastructure-has-historically-promoted-inequality.

22. Christopher Robbins, "Robert Caro Wonders What New York Is Going to

Become," *Gothamist*, February 17, 2016, https://gothamist.com/news/robert-caro-wonders-what-new-york-is-going-to-become.

23. Farrell Evans, "How Interstate Highways Gutted Communities—and Reinforced Segregation," *History*, October 20, 2021, https://www.history.com/news/interstate-highway-system-infrastructure-construction-segregation.

24. Ryan Lugalia-Hollon and Daniel Cooper, *The War on Neighborhoods: Policing, Prison, and Punishment in a Divided City* (Boston: Beacon Press, 2018).

25. Dezmond Goff, in discussion with the author, September 2020.

26. It was only after the massive real estate acquisitions of the Great Recession that single-family homes became rental properties. Richard Florida, "How Housing Wealth Transferred from Families to Corporations," *Bloomberg*, October 4, 2019, https://www.bloomberg.com/news/articles/2019-10-04/the-decline-in-owner-occupied-single-family-homes.

27. Surya Deva and Leilani Farha, OL OTH 17/2019, Letter to Stephen Schwarzman, March 22, 2019, https://www.ohchr.org/sites/default/files/Documents/Issues/Housing/Financialization/OL_OTH_17_2019.pdf.

28. Nathalie Baptiste, "Staggering Loss of Black Wealth Due to Subprime Scandal Continues Unabated," *The American Prospect*, October 13, 2014, https://prospect.org/justice/staggering-loss-black-wealth-due-subprime-scandal-continues-unabated.

29. Tim Henderson, "Investors Bought a Quarter of Homes Sold Last Year, Driving Up Rents," Pew Charitable Trusts, July 22, 2022, https://www.pewtrusts.org/en/research-and-analysis/blogs/stateline/2022/07/22/investors-bought-a-quarter-of-homes-sold-last-year-driving-up-rents.

30. Desiree Fields and Elora Raymond, "Housing Financialization and Racial Capitalism After the Global Financial Crisis," in *Housing Justice in Unequal Cities*, ed. Ananya Roy and Hilary Malson (Los Angeles: Institute on Inequality and Democracy, December 2016), 146, https://unequalcities.org/2019/10/15/housing-justice-in-unequal-cities.

31. While neoliberalism is used pejoratively to refer to any number of features of contemporary capitalism, the term here refers to the capitalist state actively constructing markets, rather than withdrawing from them, as in laissez-faire economic liberalism. Michel Foucault, *The Birth of Biopolitics: Lectures at the Collège de France, 1978–79*, ed. Michel Senellart, trans. Graham Burchell (Hampshire: Palgrave McMillan, 2008), 120–21.

32. City of San Francisco Budget and Legislative Analyst's Office, "Report to Supervisor Preston re: Residential Vacancies in San Francisco," January 31, 2022, https://sfgov.legistar.com/View.ashx?M=F&ID=10441217&GUID=3331928E-0574-4AEA-90DB-35D04F638EDB; Adam Brinklow, "San Francisco Has Nearly Five Empty Homes Per Homeless Resident," *Curbed San Francisco*, December 3, 2019,

https://sf.curbed.com/2019/12/3/20993251/san-francisco-bay-area-vacant
-homes-per-homeless-count.

33. Ted Andersen, "It Looks Like Steph Curry Didn't Buy a Unit at S.F.'S Four Seasons Residences After All. Few Others Have, Either," *San Francisco Business Times*, October 26, 2022, https://www.bizjournals.com/sanfrancisco/news/2022/10/26/four-seasons-sf-condo-sales-mission-st-steph-curry.html.

34. Derek Thompson, "Why Manhattan's Skyscrapers Are Empty," *The Atlantic*, January 16, 2020, https://www.theatlantic.com/ideas/archive/2020/01/american-housing-has-gone-insane/605005.

35. Manuel B. Aalbers, Rodrigo Fernandez, and Gertjan Wijburg, "The Financialization of Real Estate," in *The Routledge International Handbook of Financialization*, ed. Philip Mader, Daniel Mertens, and Natascha van Der Zwan (London: Routledge, 2020), 202.

36. P.E. Moscowitz, *How to Kill a City: Gentrification, Inequality, and the Fight for the Neighborhood* (New York: Nation Books, 2017), chap. 2, EPUB.

37. The gentrification economy does not produce gentrification everywhere: post-industrial desolation, exurban sprawl, and the brown muck of Congolese coltan mines are its products, as well. It does, however, incentivize urban displacement from its centers of wealth to an unprecedented degree. Gentrification is the "rational" product of the tech economy.

38. Mike Davis, *Planet of Slums* (London: Verso Books, 2007), 107.

39. Andrew Lee, "Learning to Swim in the Bay," *Notes from Below*, July 1, 2020, https://notesfrombelow.org/article/learning-swim-bay.

I. SPACE

1. Issi Romem and Elizabeth Kneebone, *Disparity in Departure: Who Leaves the Bay Area and Where Do They Go?* (Berkeley: Terner Center for Housing Innovation, 2018), https://ternercenter.berkeley.edu/wp-content/uploads/pdfs/Disparity_in_Departure.pdf.

2. Danielle Echeverria, "Only One U.S. City Saw a Bigger Pandemic Exodus Than San Francisco," *San Francisco Chronicle*, June 18, 2021, https://www.sfchronicle.com/local/article/Only-one-U-S-city-saw-a-bigger-pandemic-exodus-16258720.php.

3. Emilio Granados Franco, Richard Lukacs, and Robert Muggah, "Here's How Rising Global Risks Will Change Our Cities," World Economic Forum, January 21, 2021, https://www.weforum.org/agenda/2021/01/how-we-live-and-work-will-change-so-will-the-cities-we-inhabit/.

4. Raj Jayadev, "Electronics Assembly for Poverty Wages: Behind Silicon Valley's Instant Millionaires," *Labor Notes*, October 3, 1999, https://www.labornotes.org/1999/10/electronics-assembly-poverty-wages-behind-silicon-valleys-instant-millionaires.

5. David Bacon, "Roots of Social Justice Organizing in Silicon Valley," *Race, Poverty and the Environment*, 2016, https://www.reimaginerpe.org/20-2/bacon-Valley-social-justice-organizing.

6. Karl Marx and Friedrich Engels, trans. L.M. Findlay, *The Communist Manifesto* (Peterborough: Broadview Press, 2004), 66, 70.

7. Against the stereotype of the male industrial worker, the workforce of the early Industrial Revolution was predominantly female. The Watham-Lowell factory system in New England, for example, exclusively recruited young white women. In 1836, the Lowell Factory Girls Association staged a strike of twenty-five hundred workers. While the archetypal proletarian in the "race-blind" white imaginary is white, the wealth and productive capacity of the contemporary United States was clearly constructed by the super-exploitation of workers of color within and outside its borders, female workers of color most of all. The conception of the archetypal worker as a white man is both politically noxious and demonstrably false.

8. Guy Debord, Attila Kotányi, and Raoul Vaneigem, "Theses on the Paris Commune," in *Situationist International Anthology*, ed. Ken Knabb (Berkeley: Bureau of Public Secrets, 2006), 399.

9. Wealth-X, World Ultra Wealth Report 2021, June 2021, https://go.wealthx.com/world-ultra-wealth-report-2021.

10. Andrew DePietro, "20 Cities with the Biggest Growth in Income over the Last Decade," *Forbes*, April 29, 2021, https://www.forbes.com/sites/andrewdepietro/2021/04/29/20-cities-with-the-biggest-growth-in-income-over-the-last-decade.

11. Eric He, "A $9,000 Mortgage in San Jose? That's 'Reasonable,' Realtors Say," *San José Spotlight*, June 29, 2022, https://sanjosespotlight.com/a-9000-mortgage-in-san-jose-thats-reasonable-realtors-say.

12. U.S. Census Bureau, American Community Survey 1-Year Subject Tables, Occupation by Sex for the Civilian Employed Population 16 Years and Over, 2019, https://data.census.gov.

13. Michaela D. Platzer, John F. Sargent Jr., and Karen M. Sutter, *Semiconductors: U.S. Industry, Global Competition, and Federal Policy* (Washington, DC: Congressional Research Service, 2020), 24, https://crsreports.congress.gov/product/pdf/R/R46581/4; National People's Congress, *Outline of the People's Republic of China 14th Five-Year Plan for National Economic and Social Development and Long-Range Objectives for 2035*, trans. Ben Murphy (Washington, DC: Center for Security and Emerging Technology, 2021), 7, https://cset.georgetown.edu/publication/china-14th-five-year-plan.

14. Andrew Lee, "Lack of Housing Is Not the Problem," *Yes! Magazine*, August 10, 2021, https://www.yesmagazine.org/issue/how-much-is-enough/2021/08/10/fair-housing-affordable-land.

15. "Bay Area Housing Crisis: This Woman Lives in a Closet in San Francisco's Alamo Square Neighborhood," *ABC7 News*, July 31, 2019, https://abc7news .com/sf-closet-house-woman-lives-in-home-alamo-square/5422628.

16. Conor Dougherty, "12 People in a 3-Bedroom House, Then the Virus Entered the Equation," *New York Times*, August 1, 2020, https://www.nytimes.com /2020/08/01/business/economy/housing-overcrowding-coronavirus.html.

17. Emerald, in discussion with the author, October 2021.

18. W. Richard Scott and Michael W. Kirst, *Higher Education and Silicon Valley: Connected but Conflicted* (Baltimore, Johns Hopkins University Press, 2017), 161; Abhiram Rishi Prattipati, "Academic Senate Supports Student Safety in Overnight Parking Resolution," *La Voz News*, April 6, 2019, https:// lavozdeanza.com/news/2019/04/06/academic-senate-supports-student -safety-in-overnight-parking-resolution/.

19. Miranda Leitsinger, "After Mountain View Approves RV Ban, Housing Advocates Vow to Fight it at Ballot Box," *KQED*, October 23, 2019, https:// www.kqed.org/news/11782096/after-mountain-view-approves-rv-ban -housing-advocates-vow-to-fight-it-at-ballot-box.

20. Liz González, in discussion with the author, September 2020.

21. Enrico Moretti, *The New Geography of Jobs* (Boston: Houghton Mifflin Harcourt, 2012), 153.

22. Dora Apel, "The Ruins of Capitalism," *Jacobin*, June 2015, https://jacobin .com/2015/06/ruin-porn-imagery-photography-detroit; People who distinguish between "high-skilled" and "low-skilled" jobs should first attempt to work ten hours on an electronics assembly line or survive a dish pit during a Saturday night dinner rush. Since such people believe the latter jobs require only minimal skill, they should naturally excel. What actually distinguishes these two types of jobs is not skill but compensation, demographics, and whether the necessary knowledge and practices are acquired on the job or at a separate educational institution. Those who receive more justify the poverty of others by imagining it is due to differences in an abstract variable called "skill," which we happen to measure only by counting the years of formal education a job requires. Little wonder that by this standard, emerging as it does from academic literature, it is professors who have the most skill of all.

23. Robert R. Ebert, "Studebaker Announces Plans to Abandon U.S. Auto Production," in *Chronology of Twentieth-Century Business and Commerce*, Vol. II, ed. Frank N. Magill (London: Routledge, 2013), 832.

24. Breana Noble, "Grand Plan to Redevelop Packard Plant Is Scrapped; Eyesore Goes Back on Market," *The Detroit News*, October 29, 2020, https:// www.detroitnews.com/story/business/2020/10/29/grand-plan-redevelop -packard-plant-ruins-in-detroit-scrapped/6076466002; "About," *Michigan*

Central (website), accessed August 21, 2021, https://michigancentral.com/about.

25. "Master Innovation and Development Plan," Sidewalk Labs, 2019, 26, 30, 34, https://www.sidewalklabs.com/toronto.

26. Sidewalk Labs, 423.

27. Sidewalk Labs, 425, 430.

28. Freeman, *There Goes the 'Hood*, 2.

29. Shoshana Zuboff, *The Age of Surveillance Capitalism: The Fight for a Human Future at the New Frontier of Power* (New York: Public Affairs, 2019), 227; Shoshana Zuboff, "Toronto is Surveillance Capitalism's New Frontier," *Toronto Life*, September 4, 2019, https://torontolife.com/city/toronto-is-surveillance-capitalisms-new-frontier.

30. "FAQs," Block Sidewalk, retrieved August. 23, 2021 (site discontinued).

31. Leyland Cecco, "Google Affiliate Sidewalk Labs Abruptly Abandons Toronto Smart City Project," *The Guardian*, May 7, 2020, https://www.theguardian.com/technology/2020/may/07/google-sidewalk-labs-toronto-smart-city-abandoned.

32. "Enough. It's Time to Block Sidewalk Labs for Good," Block Sidewalk, October 31, 2019 (site discontinued).

33. The same effect is created by business districts composed of smaller firms or expanding university campuses.

34. Frantz Fanon, *The Wretched of the Earth*, trans. Constance Farrington (New York: Grove Weidenfeld, 1963), 37.

35. Emerald, in discussion with the author, November 2021.

36. Giorgio Agamben, *Homo Sacer*, trans. Daniel Heller-Roazen (Stanford: Stanford University Press, 1998), 24.

37. Carla Yanni, *Living on Campus: An Architectural History of the American Dormitory* (Minneapolis: University of Minnesota Press: 2019).

38. Steven J. Diner, *Universities and Their Cities: Urban Higher Education in America* (Baltimore: Johns Hopkins University Press, 2017), 4.

39. "Facebook's Gorgeous New Campus Has a 'Green Roof' the Size of 7 Football Fields," *Time*, March 30, 2015, https://time.com/3763880/facebook-campus-grass-roof.

40. Agustin Chevez and DJ Huppatz, "The Rise of the Corporate Campus," *The Conversation*, September 26, 2017, https://theconversation.com/the-rise-of-the-corporate-campus-84370.

41. Neil Smith, *The New Urban Frontier: Gentrification and the Revanchist City* (London: Routledge, 1999), 144.

42. Neil Smith, "Towards a Theory of Gentrification: A Back to the City Movement of Capital, Not People," *Journal of the American Planning Association* vol. 45, no. 4 (1979): 545.

43. Andre M. Perry, Jonathan Rothwell, and David Harshbarger, "The Devaluation of Assets in Black Neighborhoods: The Case of Residential Property," Brookings Institution, November 27, 2018, https://www.brookings.edu/research/devaluation-of-assets-in-black-neighborhoods.

44. Vasudha, in discussion with the author, September 2021.

45. "Distribution of Google Employees in the United States from 2014 to 2021, by Ethnicity," Statista, https://www.statista.com/statistics/311810/google-employee-ethnicity-us.

46. Daniel José Older, "Gentrification's Insidious Violence: The Truth about American Cities," Salon, April 8, 2014, https://www.salon.com/2014/04/08/gentrifications_insidious_violence_the_truth_about_american_cities.

47. Robert Garrova, "In Los Angeles, Mariachi Musicians Fight Gentrification to Keep Tradition Alive," Marketplace, September 15, 2017, https://www.marketplace.org/2017/09/15/los-angeles-mariachi-musicians-fight-gentrification-keep-tradition.

48. Andrew Zaleski, "'The Great Inversion': Cites Are the New Suburbs, Suburbs Are the New Cities," The Grist, May 30, 2012, https://grist.org/cities/the-great-inversion-cities-are-the-new-suburbs-suburbs-the-new-cities.

49. Alan Ehrenhalt, The Great Inversion and the Future of the American City (New York: Random House, 2012), 15.

50. Samuel Stein, Capital City: Gentrification and the Real Estate State (London: Verso, 2019), 60.

51. Mike Davis, Prisoners of the American Dream: Politics and Economy in the History of the U.S. Working Class (London: Verso, 1999), 119.

52. Both cities take advantage of a state-enforced disparity in wages and limitations on mobility between them and a neighboring city: El Paso and Hong Kong. It is notable that many gentrifying cities in the United States have concentrations of tech, research, and finance firms but lack a corresponding industrial city on the opposite side of a shared border.

53. Wendy Brown, Walled States, Waning Sovereignty (Brooklyn: Zone Books, 2010).

54. Grace Lee Boggs, "Grace Lee Boggs: Small Rebellions," interview by Michelle Chen, Guernica, July 15, 2014, https://www.guernicamag.com/small-rebellions.

55. Allen J. Scott, Global City-Regions: Trends, Theory, Policy (Oxford: Oxford University Press, 2001), 1.

56. Scott, Global City-Regions, 13.

57. Smith, The New Urban Frontier, 37.

58. Neil Harvey, "Las Fuerzas de Liberación Nacional y la Guerra Fría en México 1969–1974," talk given at the Casa Museo de la Memoria Histórico, July

15, 2015, http://casadetodasytodos.org/dialogos/las-fuerzas-de-liberacion
-nacional-y-la-guerra-fria-en-mexico-1969-1974-sumario.

59.	Antony Beevor, *The Battle for Spain: The Spanish Civil War, 1936–1939* (New
York: Penguin Books, 2006), 112, 105.

60.	Maurice Meisner, *Mao Zedong: A Political and Intellectual Portrait* (Cam-
bridge: Polity Press, 2007), 16, 50.

61.	Meisner, *Mao Zedong*, 53.

62.	The inclusion of authoritarian state socialist as well as anarchist and neo-
zapatista revolutionary formations is not meant to paper over severe strategic and political divisions between them. Such tendencies are included to
recognize their shared historic opposition to the bourgeois state and capitalist social relations. The resounding failures of "socialist governments" to
build communism does not negate the fact that many participants in these
movements made enormous sacrifices in earnest efforts to abolish capitalism and the institution of the state that reproduces it—often paying with
their lives. They include those sympathetic to anarchism, such as Cuba's
Camilo Cienfuegos, as well as anarchists like Peter Kropotkin, who gave
enthusiastic support to the October Revolution before later critiquing Bol-
shevik "party dictatorship," and Lucy Parsons, who collaborated with the
CPUSA in the late 1930s.

63.	Philadelphia Housing Action, "Release: Philadelphia Housing Action
Claims Victory After 6 Month Direct Action Campaign Forces City to Relin-
quish 50 Vacant Homes to Community Land Trust," September 26, 2020,
https://philadelphiahousingaction.info/release-philadelphia-housing
-action-claims-victory-after-6-month-direct-action-campaign-forces-city
-to-relinquish-50-vacant-homes-to-community-land-trust.

64.	Ben Mabie and Joohyun Kim, "Strategy After Ferguson," *Viewpoint Magazine*,
February 1, 2016, https://viewpointmag.com/2016/02/01/strategy-after
-ferguson.

65.	Dave Id, "Qilombo in Oakland Evicted by Sheriff's Deputy: Chaga
Responds," *Indybay*, January 10, 2019, https://www.indybay.org/news
items/2019/01/10/18820265.php.

66.	Mable and Kim, "Strategy After Ferguson."

67.	Jennifer Sullivan, "4 Arrested and Removed from Seattle Schools' Horace
Mann Building," *The Seattle Times*, November 19, 2013, https://www.seattle
times.com/seattle-news/4-arrested-and-removed-from-seattle-schools
-horace-mann-building.

68.	Dezmond Goff, in discussion with the author, September 2020.

69.	Andrew Lee, "Lack of Housing is Not the Problem," *Yes! Magazine*, August
10, 2021, https://www.yesmagazine.org/issue/how-much-is-enough
/2021/08/10/fair-housing-affordable-land.

70. John Greenfield, "Activists Worry CTA-Friendly Housing Will Accelerate Logan Square Gentrification," *Chicago Reader*, April 18, 2016, https://chicagoreader.com/columns-opinion/activists-worry-cta-friendly-housing-will-accelerate-logan-square-gentrification.

71. Melissa Checker, "Wiped Out by the 'Greenwave': Environmental Gentrification and the Paradoxical Politics of Urban Sustainability," *City & Society* 23 no. 2 (2011): 210–29.

72. Laura Kiesel, "Why 'Greening' Cities Can Make Gentrification Worse—And Often Doesn't Help the Environment Either," *Salon*, February 26, 2022, https://www.salon.com/2022/02/26/eco-gentrification.

73. Elizabeth Kneebone and Natalie Holmes, "The Growing Distance between People and Jobs in Metropolitan America," Brookings Institution, March 24, 2015, https://www.brookings.edu/research/the-growing-distance-between-people-and-jobs-in-metropolitan-america.

74. Erin Baldassari, "Stretching the Boundaries," *The Mercury News*, February 17, 2019, https://extras.mercurynews.com/megaregion.

75. Jenna, in discussion with the author, September 2021.

76. Círculo de Comunistas Esotéricos, *Tiempos Mejores: Tesis Provisionales Sobre la Revuelta de Octubre de 2019* (Santiago: Comunistas Esotéricos, 2019), 19, https://comunistasesotericos.noblogs.org/files/2020/03/Tiempos-Mejores-1.pdf.

77. Michael Janoschka and Antoine Casgrain, *Urbanismo Neoliberal y Gentrificación en Santiago de Chile: Diálogos entre Teoría Urbana y Reivindicación Vecinal* (Santiago: Movimiento de Pobladores en Lucha, 2012).

78. Michael Hogan, "Latin American Gentrification: The Case of Santiago," *Carolina Planning Journal ANGLES*, April 20, 2016, https://carolinaangles.com/2016/04/20/latin-american-gentrification-the-case-of-santiago.

79. Adrián G. Aguilar and Peter Ward, "Globalization, Regional Development, and Mega-City Expansion in Latin America: Analyzing Mexico City's Peri-Urban Hinterland," *Cities* 20, no. 1 (2002): 4.

80. "Cars, Guns, Autonomy: On the Finer Points of the Recent Revolt in Ferguson, MO," *Avalanche* no. 4 (November, 2019): 18–23.

81. "Revolt and Recuperation: Avenging George Floyd," *Confrontaciones*, July 20, 2020, https://confrontacionesblog.noblogs.org/thebattleofsanjose.

82. Jenna, in discussion with the author, September 2021.

83. Círculo de Comunistas Esotéricos, *Tiempos Mejores*, 23.

II. PLACE

1. Yi-Fu Tuan, *Space and Place: The Perspective of Experience* (Minneapolis: University of Minnesota Press, 1977), 12.

2. Jennifer Swann, "The Fight over the First Baptist Church of

Venice," *Curbed Los Angeles*, December 15, 2017, https://la.curbed.com /2017/12/15/16780810/first-baptist-church-venice-jay-penske.

3. Bridgette M. Redman, "We Were All Here: New Film Captures History of Santa Monica's Pico Neighborhood and Casillas Family," *The Argonaut*, June 23, 2021, https://www.argonautnews.com/arts-events/we-were-all-here/ article_eb29c1fd-9cad-5427-b749-6a6e113f4eb0.html.

4. Jataun Valentine, in discussion with the author, September 2020.

5. Deborah Hastings, "Venice's Oakwood District: 'Los Angeles at its Worst,'" *Los Angeles Sentinel*, January 27, 1994.

6. Gary Walker, "In Venice While Black," *The Argonaut*, November 18, 2015, https://www.argonautnews.com/news/in-venice-while-black/article _06ecc4df-bb29-5477-b3f6-2ce6b669938a.html.

7. Martha Groves and Lisa Richardson, "Wealth, Poverty, Anger Live Together in Venice," *Los Angeles Times*, June 9, 2006, https://www.latimes.com/ archives/la-xpm-2006-jun-09-me-venice9-story.html.

8. Swann, "The Fight over the First Baptist Church."

9. Jataun Valentine, in discussion with the author, September 2020.

10. Jon Wolff, "Save Venice Wins Historic Designation for the First Baptist Church of Venice," *Free Venice Beachhead*, October 15, 2021, https://the venicebeachhead.com/2021/10/15/save-venice-wins-historic-designation -for-the-first-baptist-church-of-venice.

11. Nicole Charky, "Venice Historic Black Church Recommended for Monu- ment Status," *Patch*, June 4, 2021, https://patch.com/california/venice/ venice-historic-black-church-recommended-monument-status.

12. Jeremy Divinity, "A Tale of Two Venices: Before There Was Dogtown, There Was Oakwood," *Knock LA*, July 9, 2020, https://knock-la.com/venice -oakwood-black-neighborhood-history-a270785f0a04.

13. J.M. Valle, "The Mural de La Raza Was My Mirror," *Silicon Valley De-Bug*, January 14, 2019, https://siliconvalleydebug.org/stories/the-mural-de-la -raza-was-my-mirror.

14. Leonardo Castañeda, "'Mural Free': Conspiracy Alleged in East San Jose Mural Lawsuit," *The Mercury News*, March 6, 2019, https://www.mercury news.com/2019/03/06/mural-free-conspiracy-alleged-in-east-san-jose -mural-lawsuit.

15. J.M. Valle, "The Mural de La Raza."

16. Tatiana Sanchez, "Mysterious Removal of Historic San Jose Mural Sparks $5 Million Lawsuit," *The Mercury News*, November 5, 2018, https:// www.mercurynews.com/2018/11/05/mysterious-removal-of-historic -san-jose-mural-sparks-5-million-lawsuit.

17. Vasudha, in discussion with the author, September 2021.

18. Bryan Peraza, in discussion with the author, September 2021.

19.   Erualdo R. González and Carolina S. Sarmiento, "The Gentrification of Santa Ana: From Origin to Resistance," *KCET*, September 13, 2017, https://www.kcet.org/shows/city-rising/the-gentrification-of-santa-ana-from-origin-to-resistance.

20.   David Carbajal Torres, in discussion with the author, October 2021.

21.   Andrew Lee, "Defend Community: David (Tú Santa Ana) on Tenant Resistance," *Anti-Racism Daily*, November 3, 2021, https://the-ard.com/2021/11/03/defend-community-david-tu-santa-ana-on-tenant-resistance.

22.   A resident of Colonia Juárez.

23.   Víctor Delgadillo, "Una Santa Anti-gentrificadora en la Ciudad de México," *El País*, February 27, 2017, https://elpais.com/elpais/2017/02/23/seres_urbanos/1487839044_932988.html.

24.   Shelma Navarette, "¿Y el Corredor Cultural Chapultepec? La Pregunta de los 921 Millones," *Expansión Política*, July 19, 2019, https://politica.expansion.mx/cdmx/2019/07/19/y-el-corredor-cultural-chapultepec-la-pregunta-de-los-921-millones.

25.   Alison Bell, "The Anti-Google Alliance," *Exberliner*, March 29, 2018, https://www.exberliner.com/politics/the-anti-google-alliance.

26.   Daniel González, in discussion with the author, September 2020.

27.   Yi-Fu Tuan, *Space and Place*, 12.

28.   Leonardo Castañeda, "San José's disappearing murals: 'It's like wiping away people's history,'" *The Mercury News*, December 16, 2018, https://www.mercurynews.com/2018/12/16/san-joses-disappearing-murals-its-like-wiping-away-peoples-history.

29.   Noni Session, in discussion with the author, May 2021.

30.   Charles Baudelaire, "The Eyes of the Poor," *Paris Spleen: Little Poems in Prose*, trans. Keith Waldrop (Middletown: Wesleyan University Press, 209), 52.

31.   Mike Davis, *Planet of Slums* (London: Verso Books, 2007), 101.

32.   San José Arts Advocates, "Community Visioning Workshop Minutes," November 11, 2020.

33.   González and Sarmiento, "The Gentrification of Santa Ana."

34.   "UNESCO, Airbnb and Mexico City Partner to Promote the City as a Remote Working Hub," Airbnb, October 25, 2022, https://news.airbnb.com/cdmx-unesco-and-airbnb-announce-partnerships-to-promote-mexico-city-as-a-g/.

35.   Jaylinn Herrera, "More Americans Are Living and Working in Mexico. Where Does That Leave the Locals?" *NBC News*, November 12, 2022, https://www.nbcnews.com/news/latino/more-americans-living-mexico-effects-locals-rents-rcna56662.

36.   Inga Saffron, "Racing Against Time to Save South Philadelphia's 'Black Main Street,'" *The Philadelphia Inquirer*, May 30, 2021, https://www.

inquirer.com/columnists/black-doctors-row-christian-street-south-phil-adelphia-main-preservation-architecture-julian-abele-frederick-mas-siah-20210530.html.

37. Inga Saffron, "The Real Problem with Gentrification," *The New Republic*, February 15, 2013, https://newrepublic.com/article/112422/gentrifica-tions-real-problem-monotony.

38. Faye Anderson, "Gentrifiers and Black History in Philadelphia Update," *All That Philly Jazz*, June 27, 2021, https://phillyjazz.us/2021/06/27/doctors -row-christian-street-historic-district-preservation-alliance-for-greater -philadelphia-gentrification-displacement-black-history.

39. Guy Debord, *Society of the Spectacle*, trans. Donald Nicholson-Smith (Brooklyn: Zone Books, 2020), 12.

40. James Baldwin, *Nobody Knows My Name: More Notes of a Native Son* (New York: Vintage International, 1993), 217.

41. Charles W. Mills, "White Ignorance," in *Race and Epistemologies of Ignorance*, ed. Shannon Sullivan and Nancy Tuana (Albany: State University of New York Press, 2007), 11–38.

42. James C. Scott, *Seeing Like a State* (New Haven: Yale University Press, 1998), 2.

43. Nikil Saval, "The Office and the City," in *City by City: Dispatches from the American Metropolis*, ed. Keith Gessen and Stephen Squibb (New York: n+1/Farrar, Straus and Giroux, 2015), 72.

44. Smith, *The New Urban Frontier*, 24.

45. Smith, *The New Urban Frontier*, 9; Holland Cotter, "When the Young Lords Were Outlaws in New York," *New York Times*, July 23, 2015, https://www .nytimes.com/2015/07/24/arts/design/when-the-young-lords-strove-to -change-new-york.html.

46. Jennifer Rosdale, "The Quad: A Newly Defined Meta-Hood," Jennifer Ros-dail Real Estate Team, March 7, 2014, https://www.jenniferrosdail.com/ the-quad-is-born.

47. Adam Allington, "If Your Neighborhood's Name Changes, It's Probably Being Gentrified," *Marketplace*, July 18, 2017, https://www.marketplace.org /2017/07/18/neighborhood-rebranding-prompts-gentrification-worries; Harriet Alexander, "Bronx Gentrification Leaves New Yorkers Up in Arms," *The Telegraph*, November 17, 2015, https://www.telegraph.co.uk/news/ worldnews/northamerica/usa/11999467/Bronx-gentrification-leaves-New -Yorkers-up-in-arms.html.

48. Darwin BondGraham, "Gentrification Changed the Names of Oak-land Neighborhoods," *East Bay Express*, September 19, 2018, https://east bayexpress.com/gentrification-changed-the-names-of-oakland-neighbor hoods-2-1.

49. "Tenderloin May Be 'Union Square West' Of The Future," *KPIX* 5, October 24, 2016, https://www.cbsnews.com/sanfrancisco/news/real-estate-firm -looks-to-re-brand-tenderloin-neighborhood-as-union-square-west.

50. Rachael A. Portelli, "What Happens When Big Business Tries to Rename a Neighborhood?," *Seattle Star*, April 27, 2019, https://www.seattlestar.net/2019 /04/what-happens-when-big-business-tries-to-rename-a-neighborhood.

51. John L. Puckett, "The University City Science Center and the Black Bottom," *West Philadelphia Collaborative History*, https://collaborativehistory .gse.upenn.edu/stories/university-city-science-center-and-black-bottom.

52. Anna Orso, "How 'Pennification' Turned Black Bottom into University City, and Changed the Neighborhood Forever," *Billy Penn*, August 5, 2015, https:// billypenn.com/2015/08/05/how-penntrification-turned-black-bottom-into -university-city-and-changed-the-neighborhood-forever.

53. Taylor Allen, "As Building Boom Continues in West Philly, Black Bottom Tribe Fights for a Sign of the Community They Lost," *WHYY*, August 9, 2021, https://whyy.org/articles/as-building-boom-continues-in-west-philly -black-bottom-tribe-fights-for-a-sign-of-the-community-they-lost.

54. Andrew Lee, "Fighting 'Penn-ification' with the People's Townhomes," *Anti-Racism Daily*, September 22, 2022, https://the-ard.com/2022/09/22/ fighting-penn-ification-with-the-peoples-townhomes.

55. Jaclyn Lee, "UC Townhomes Residents Present Plan to Purchase Complex, Demand More Affordable Housing," *6 ABC*, September 8, 2022, https://6abc.com/philadelphia-pa-uc-townhomes-west-philly-affordable -housing/12210467.

56. Claudio Milano and José A. Mansilla, *Ciudad de Vacaciones: Conflictos Urbanos en Espacios Turísticos* (Barcelona: Pol-len Edicions, 2019), 48–55.

57. Helen V.S. Cole, Roshanak Mehdipanah, Pedro Gullón, and Margarita Triguero-Mas, "Breaking Down and Building Up: Gentrification, Its Drivers, and Urban Health Inequality," *Current Environmental Health Reports* 8 (2021): 157–66, https://doi.org/10.1007/s40572-021-00309-5.

58. "Las Dos Caras del Turismo de Barcelona," *El País*, June 30, 2017, https:// www.youtube.com/watch?v=MLH7wD6jqiw.

59. Carolyn Said, "Airbnb Profits Prompted S.F. Eviction, Ex-Tenant Says," *SFGate*, January 22, 2014, https://www.sfgate.com/bayarea/article/Airbnb -profits-prompted-S-F-eviction-ex-tenant-5164242.php.

60. Josh Bivens, "The Economic Costs and Benefits of Airbnb," *Economic Policy Institute*, January 30, 2019, 2, https://files.epi.org/pdf/157766.pdf.

61. Senay Boztas, "Airbnb Is Accused Of Destroying Cities. This Company Says It's The Ethical Alternative," *Huffington Post*, June 2, 2019, https://www .huffpost.com/entry/airbnb-affordable-housing-gentrification-tourism -fairbnb_n_5c5949c3e4b00187b554828d.

62. Debord, *Society of the Spectacle*, 168.

63. Stephen Gibbs, "Cuba Recognises the Right to Buy and Sell Property," *The Times*, July 17, 2018, https://www.thetimes.co.uk/article/cuba-recognises-the-right-to-buy-and-sell-property-lfjv9pbvf.

64. Chris Arsenault, "Cuba on the Verge of Illegal Property Boom as Foreign Cash Tiptoes In," *Thomson Reuters Foundation News*, January 27, 2016, https://news.trust.org/item/20160127133650-96mg8.

65. Carmen Diana Deere, "Cuba's Struggle for Self-sufficiency," *Monthly Review* 43, no. 3 (July–August 1991), https://doi.org/10.14452/MR-043-03-1991-07_4; Adrián Rodríguez B., "Gentrificación en La Habana: Los Militares, Apuestan por las 'Mudanzas' Forzosas," *Diario de Cuba*, January 7, 2019, https://diariodecuba.com/cuba/1546701655_43900.html.

66. María Karla Hernández González and Maria Tereza Duarte Paes, "Touristic Refunctionalization of the Historical Center of Old Havana," *Revisita de Geografia da UFC* 19, no. 3 (2020): 1–15, https://doi.org/10.4215/rm2020.e19020.

67. The development of biotechnology and tourism are both emphasized in Cuba's Plan Nacional de Desarrollo Económico y Social 2030, together with "measures to mitigate negative impacts" of this "transformation of production."

68. "It is, rather, a threshold in which law constantly passes over into fact and fact into law, and in which the two planes become indistinguishable." Giorgio Agamben, *Homo Sacer: Sovereign Power and Bare Life* (Stanford: Stanford University Press, 1998), 171. *Camp, campus, encampment,* and *camping* derive from the Latin word for a field used for military exercises. All refer to a site of an organized project apart from everyday life.

69. Gary Warth, "Question Persists: Are Homeless People Flocking to San Diego?" *The San Diego Union-Tribune*, June 17, 2022, https://www.sandiegouniontribune.com/news/homelessness/story/2022-06-17/question-persists-do-homeless-services-attract-homeless-people.

70. U.S. Government Accountability Office, "Better HUD Oversight of Data Collection Could Improve Estimates of Homeless Population," GAO-20-433 (2020), 30, https://www.gao.gov/products/gao-20-433.

71. Andrew Lee, "The Violence Inherent to Unhoused Encampment Sweeps," *Anti-Racism Daily*, August 12, 2022, https://the-ard.com/2022/08/15/the-violence-inherent-in-encampment-sweeps.

72. Matthew Weaver, "New York Gives Homeless People a One-Way Ticket To Leave City," *The Guardian*, July 29, 2009, https://www.theguardian.com/world/2009/jul/29/new-york-homeless-ticket-leave.

73. Joe Kukura, "Does Giving Bus Tickets Out of Town Really Help the Homeless? The Chronicle Crunches The Numbers," *SFist*, July 29, 2019, https://

sfist.com/2019/07/29/does-giving-bus-tickets-out-of-town-really-help-the-homeless-the-chron-crunches-the-numbers.

74.   Eben Blake, "Homeless Bus Ticket Programs Across the Nation Offer Little Accountability, Poor Housing Solutions, Activists Say," *International Business Times*, January 24, 2015, https://www.ibtimes.com/homeless-bus-ticket-programs-across-nation-offer-little-accountability-poor-housing-2016812.

75.   Lisa "Tiny" Gray-García, in discussion with the author, December 2022.

76.   Andrew Lee, "The Violence Inherent in Encampment Sweeps," *Anti-Racism Daily*, August 15, 2022, https://the-ard.com/2022/08/15/the-violence-inherent-in-encampment-sweeps.

77.   Sandy Perry, in discussion with the author, June 2021.

III. LABOR

1.   Joe Fitzgerald Rodriguez, "SB 827 Rallies End with Yimbys Shouting Down Protestors of Color," *San Francisco Examiner*, April 5, 2018, https://www.sfexaminer.com/news/sb-827-rallies-end-with-yimbys-shouting-down-protesters-of-color/article_42f1bb0c-c4c5-5401-a395-5aff1b28137c.html.

2.   Sonja Trauss, "Does Adding Expensive Housing Help the Little Guy?" *Market Urbanism Report*, July 3, 2018, https://marketurbanismreport.com/blog/does-adding-expensive-housing-help-the-little-guy.

3.   Julia Carrie Wong, "The Mission Moratorium and the Other Bubble," *SF Weekly*, June 3, 2015, https://www.sfweekly.com/news/the-mission-moratorium-and-the-other-bubble.

4.   Mark O'Connell, "Why Silicon Valley Billionaires Are Prepping for the Apocalypse in New Zealand," *The Guardian*, February 15, 2018, https://www.theguardian.com/news/2018/feb/15/why-silicon-valley-billionaires-are-prepping-for-the-apocalypse-in-new-zealand.

5.   Trauss, "Expensive Housing."

6.   Patrick Sisson, "Why Do All New Apartment Buildings Look the Same?" *Curbed*, December 4, 2018, https://archive.curbed.com/2018/12/4/18125536/real-estate-modern-apartment-architecture.

7.   Justin Fox, "Why America's New Apartment Buildings All Look the Same," *Bloomberg Businessweek*, February 13, 2019, https://www.bloomberg.com/news/features/2019-02-13/why-america-s-new-apartment-buildings-all-look-the-same.

8.   Jerusalem Demsas, "In Defense of the 'Gentrification Building,'" *Vox*, September 10, 2021, https://www.vox.com/22650806/gentrification-affordable-housing-low-income-housing.

9.   J. Revel Sims, "Measuring the Effect of Gentrification on Displacement: Multifamily Housing and Eviction in Wisconsin's Madison Urban Region,"

Housing Policy Debate 31 (2021): 736–61, https://doi.org/10.1080/10511482.2
021.1871931.

10.   Yonah Freemark, "Upzoning Chicago: Impacts of a Zoning Reform on
Property Values and Housing Construction," *Urban Affairs Review* 56, no. 3
(2020): 758–89, https://doi.org/10.1177/1078087418824672.

11.   Anthony Damiano and Chris Frenier, "Build Baby Build?: Housing Sub-
markets and the Effects of New Construction on Existing Rents," *Center
for Urban and Regional Affairs*, October 6, 2020, https://www.tonydamiano
.com/project/new-con/bbb-wp.pdf.

12.   Karen Chapple, et al., *Housing Market Interventions and Residential Mobility
in the San Francisco Bay Area*, Federal Reserve Bank of San Francisco, WP
2022-1 (2022).

13.   Liz González, in discussion with the author, May 2021.

14.   David Carbajal Torres, in discussion with the author, October 2021.

15.   Esteban Rossi-Hanberg, Pierre-Daniel Sarte, and Felipe Schwartzman, *Cog-
nitive Hubs and Spatial Redistribution*, Federal Reserve Bank of Richmond,
WP 19-16 (2019), 37, https://www.richmondfed.org/-/media/Richmond
FedOrg/publications/research/working_papers/2019/wp19-16.pdf.

16.   Vasudha, in discussion with the author, September 2021.

17.   Tracy Rosenthal, "101 Notes on the LA Tenants Union," *Commune*, July 19,
2019, https://communemag.com/101-notes-on-the-la-tenants-union.

18.   Avi Asher-Schapiro, "Move Fast and Build Solidarity," *The Nation*, March
6, 2019, https://www.thenation.com/article/archive/tech-workers-google
-facebook-protest-dsa.

19.   J.S. Tan, "Tech Workers Are Workers Too," *Collective Action in Tech*, November 17, 2020, https://collectiveaction.tech/2020/tech-workers-are-workers
-too.

20.   The truckers in the Canadian Freedom Convoy of 2022 similarly gained
leverage from the fact that their profession involved large trucks that could
be used to block streets, though few would claim that they were therefore a
union. If anything, the truckers would have the stronger claim, since they
were in part demanding a change in their work conditions in the form of the
repeal of a vaccine mandate.

21.   Guy Debord, *Society of the Spectacle*, trans. Donald Nicholson-Smith
(Brooklyn: Zone Books, 2020), 48.

22.   David Murrell, "Philly's New Generation of Unions is Young, Progressive,
and Coming to a Coffee Shop Near You," *Philadelphia Magazine*, October 17,
2020, https://www.phillymag.com/news/2020/10/17/philadelphia-unions.

23.   Isabel Togoh, "Mourners Across the U.S. Gather for What Would Have
Been George Floyd's 47th Birthday," *Forbes*, October 15, 2020 https://
www.forbes.com/sites/isabeltogoh/2020/10/15/mourners-across-the-us

-gather-for-what-would-have-been-george-floyds-47th-birthday; Larry Buchanan, Quoctrung Bui, and Jugal K. Patel, "Black Lives Matter May Be the Largest Movement in U.S. History," *New York Times*, July 3, 2020, https:// www.nytimes.com/interactive/2020/07/03/us/george-floyd-protests -crowd-size.html.

24. Lois Weiner, "How Business Unionism Got Us to Janus," *In These Times*, November 9, 2017, https://inthesetimes.com/article/janus-right-to-work -union-labor.

25. Maddy Sweitzer-Lammé, "V Street Closes Amid Workers' Attempts to Organize," *Philadelphia Magazine*, July 21, 2020, https://www.phillymag .com/foobooz/2020/07/21/v-street-closing-employee-coalition; Jenn Ladd, "Good Karma Cafe Temporarily Shutters Another Location Months after Workers Unionized," *The Philadelphia Inquirer*, July 2, 2022, https:// www.inquirer.com/news/good-karma-cafe-store-closing-coffee-shop -union-20220702.html.

26. Andrew Lee, "What Is Gentrification? How It Works, Who It Affects, And What To Do About It," *Teen Vogue*, October 20, 2020, https://www.teen vogue.com/story/what-is-gentrification-how-works.

27. Sims, "Measuring the Effect of Gentrification," 3.

28. Simone de Beauvoir, *The Second Sex*, trans. H.M. Parshley (London: Jonathan Cape, 1956), 18.

29. E.P. Thompson, *The Making of the English Working Class* (New York: Vintage Books, 1966), 11.

30. Mikhail Bakunin, "Project and Object of the Secret Revolutionary Organization of the International Brethren," in *No Gods No Masters: An Anthology of Anarchism*, ed. Daniel Guérin (Oakland: AK Press, 2005), 181.

31. Peter Kropotkin, "The Anarchist Idea," in *No Gods No Masters: An Anthology of Anarchism*, ed. Daniel Guérin (Oakland: AK Press, 2005), 277.

32. Thompson, *English Working Class*, 185.

33. Alexis de Tocqueville, *Journeys to England and Ireland*, trans. J.P. Mayer (London: Faber & Faber, 1958), 106.

34. Steven Marcus, *Engels, Manchester, and the Working Class* (New York: Random House, 1974), 6.

35. Karl Marx, *The Civil War in France*, trans. E. Belfort Bax (New York: International Library Publishing Co., 1900), 78.

36. John Gurda, *The Making of Milwaukee*, quoted by Matthew Desmond in *Evicted: Poverty and Profit in the American City* (New York: Broadway Books, 2016), 24.

37. Citibank, "The American Economy is Experiencing a Paradigm Shift," *The Atlantic*, 2018, https://www.theatlantic.com/sponsored/citi-2018/the -american-economy-is-experiencing-a-paradigm-shift/2008.

38. U.S. Census Bureau, Quarterly Workforce Indicators, https://www.census .gov/data/developers/data-sets/qwi.html. In 1994, the average monthly earnings for a worker at a firm with nineteen or fewer employees was $1,804 in 1994 and $3,593 in 2019. This includes nonemployer businesses, or self-employed people. Workers at firms with five hundred or more employees saw average monthly wages rise from $2,609 to $5,887 in the same period.

39. Jean Anyon, *Radical Possibilities: Public Policy, Urban Education, and a New Social Movement* (New York: Taylor & Francis, 2014), 97.

40. Debord, *Society of the Spectacle*, 91.

41. Klaus Schwab, "The Fourth Industrial Revolution: What It Means, How to Respond," *World Economic Forum*, January 14, 2016, https://www.weforum .org/agenda/2016/01/the-fourth-industrial-revolution-what-it-means-and -how-to-respond.

42. David Jamieson, "Amazon Union Loses Election at Staten Island Warehouse," *Huffington Post*, May 2, 2022, https://www.huffpost.com/entry/ amazon-union-loses-election-at-staten-island-warehouse_n_627017c0e4b 0cca675588edf.

43. Christopher O'Neill et al., "Burnout by Design? Warehouse and Shipping Workers Pay the Hidden Cost of the Holiday Season," *The Conversation*, November 28, 2021, https://theconversation.com/burnout-by-design -warehouse-and-shipping-workers-pay-the-hidden-cost-of-the-holiday -season-172157.

44. Andrea Iossa, "Work According to Amazon," *Equal Times*, February 22, 2018, https://www.equaltimes.org/work-according-to-amazon.

45. Alex N. Press, "Amazon Is Creating Company Towns Across the United States," *Jacobin*, July 24, 2021, https://jacobin.com/2021/07/amazon-warehouse -communities-towns-geography-warehouse-fulfillment-jfk8-cajon -inland-empire.

46. Roland Simon, "The Restructuring, as It Is in Itself," trans. MJJ, *Théorie Communiste*, https://libcom.org/library/restructuring-it-itself-roland-simon.

47. Mack DeGeurin, "Amazon Delivery Workers Threatened With Firing, Told to Keep Driving During Tornadoes," *Gizmodo*, December 17, 2021, https://gizmodo.com/amazon-delivery-workers-threatened-with-firing -told-to-1848236283; Hayley Peterson, "Missing Wages, Grueling Shifts, and Bottles of Urine: The Disturbing Accounts of Amazon Delivery Drivers May Reveal the True Human Cost of 'Free' Shipping," *Business Insider*, September 11, 2018, https://www.businessinsider.com/amazon-delivery-drivers -reveal-claims-of-disturbing-work-conditions-2018-8.

48. Michael Sainato, "14-hour Days and No Bathroom Breaks: Amazon's Overworked Delivery Drivers," *The Guardian*, March 11, 2021, https://www

.theguardian.com/technology/2021/mar/11/amazon-delivery-drivers
-bathroom-breaks-unions.

49. Sainato, "14-hour Days."

50. Mike Rosenberg and Ángel González, "Thanks to Amazon, Seattle is Now America's Biggest Company Town," *Seattle Times*, August 23, 2017, https://www.seattletimes.com/business/amazon/thanks-to-amazon-seattle-is-now-americas-biggest-company-town.

51. Quinten Dol, "Inside HQ1: The Coolest Features at Amazon's Seattle Head-quarters," *Built in Seattle*, February 5, 2020, https://www.builtinseattle.com/2019/03/08/coolest-features-amazon-seattle-headquarters; Adelaide's Cafe Menu, compass one (website), Compass Group USA, retrieved February 19, 2022, https://cafes.compass-usa.com/Amazon/Pages/Menu.aspx?lid=a46.

52. Caroline O'Donovan, "Cafeteria Workers at Intel Are Protesting," *Buzzfeed News*, February 11, 2016, https://www.buzzfeednews.com/article/caroline odonovan/cafeteria-workers-protesting-at-intel-yesterday-drew-a-crowd.

53. D, in discussion with the author, July 2022.

54. James Gallagher, Amazon Software Engineer Salary, Career Karma (website), accessed February 19, 2022, https://careerkarma.com/blog/software-engineering-salary-amazon.

55. This refers not only to syndicalism in the narrow sense, such as that of the Industrial Workers of the World, but rather a broader conception that the organization of the working class in trade unions within the workplace is an indispensable stage in the struggle for revolution or necessary reforms. Such a syndicalism forms the common sense of much of the self-described Left.

56. Lisa Rowan, "Starbucks Union: Are Labor Unions Good for Public Companies?" *Forbes Advisor*, August 30, 2022, https://www.forbes.com/advisor/investing/sbux-starbucks-union.

57. Michael Sainato, "US Graduate Students Protest Against Low Pay While Universities Profit from Their Work," *The Guardian*, March 30, 2022, https://www.theguardian.com/us-news/2022/mar/30/us-graduate-students-protest-against-low-pay-while-universities-profit-from-their-work; Laura Benshoff, "Strike by Philadelphia Museum of Art Workers Shows Woes of 'Prestige' Jobs," NPR, October 8, 2022, https://www.npr.org/2022/10/07/1127400793/what-a-strike-at-a-philadelphia-museum-reveals-about-unionizing-cultural-institu.

58. "Burger King Marquee Goes Viral with 'We All Quit' Message," *ABC 7*, July 13, 2021, https://abc7ny.com/lincoln-nebraska-sign-burger-king-rachael-flores-workers-quit/10882090; Aaron Pressman and Anissa Gardizy, "'A Giant Game of Musical Chairs': Waves of Workers Are Changing Jobs as the Pandemic Wanes," *The Boston Globe*, June 27, 2021, https://www

.bostonglobe.com/2021/06/27/business/giant-game-musical-chairs
-waves-workers-are-changing-jobs-pandemic-wanes.

59.   Jeff Cox, "Millions of people quit their jobs in the 'Great Resignation.'
      Here is why it may not last long," *CNBC*, November 18, 2021, https://www
      .cnbc.com/2021/11/18/why-the-great-resignation-may-not-last-very-long
      .html.

60.   Guy Standing, *The Precariat: The New Dangerous Class* (London: Blooms-
      bury Academic, 2011), 28.

61.   Margaret Heffernan, "What Happened After the Foxconn Suicides," *CBS
      News*, August 7, 2013, https://www.cbsnews.com/news/what-happened
      -after-the-foxconn-suicides.

62.   Michael Standaert, "This Chinese City Wants to Make Housing More
      Affordable, But . . . ," *Al Jazeera*, December 13, 2019, https://www.aljazeera
      .com/economy/2019/12/13/this-chinese-city-wants-to-make-housing
      -more-affordable-but.

63.   "Property Law of the People's Republic of China," National People's Con-
      gress of the People's Republic of China (2007), http://www.china.org.cn/
      china/LegislationsForm2001-2010/2011-02/11/content_21897791.htm;
      Pearl Liu, "Shenzhen Relaxes Rules for Developers Buying Land, Backing
      Away from the Cap That Sent Real Estate Auctions into a Tailspin," *South
      China Morning Post*, November 3, 2021, https://www.scmp.com/business/
      companies/article/3154547/shenzhen-relaxes-rules-developers-buying
      -land-backing-away-cap.

64.   Sharon Smith, "Marxism, Unions, and the Class Struggle," *International
      Socialist Review* 78 (July 2011), https://isreview.org/issue/78/marxism
      -unions-and-class-struggle; Barry Eidlin, "Why Unions Are Good—But
      Not Good Enough," *Jacobin*, January 6, 2020, https://jacobin.com/2020/01/
      marxism-trade-unions-socialism-revolutionary-organizing.

65.   To quote a particularly egregious example: "Racial discrimination towards
      Blacks is not, in our view, a central element of the exercise of capitalist
      domination. . . . [Discrimination] exists all over the world and affects all
      skin colours, all religious affiliations, all cultural or geographic origins,
      and particularly all women." Mouvement Communiste/Kolektivně proti
      Kapitálu, *"Races" and the Working Class in the USA*, Libcom.org, July 21,
      2021, https://libcom.org/article/races-and-working-class-usa-mouvement
      -communistekolektivne-proti-kapitalu-letter-48.

66.   Your Lazy Comrades, *The Interregnum: The George Floyd Uprising, the Coro-
      navirus Pandemic, and the Emerging Social Revolution, Haters Cafe*, January
      7, 2022, https://haters.noblogs.org/post/2022/01/07/the-interregnum
      -the-george-floyd-uprising-the-coronavirus-pandemic-and-the-emerging
      -social-revolution.

67. Rosa Luxemburg, "The Mass Strike," in *The Essential Rosa Luxemburg*, ed. Helen Scott (Chicago: Haymarket Books, 2008), 177.

68. Loretta Lees, Hyun Bang Shin, and Ernesto López-Morales, *Planetary Gentrification* (Cambridge: Polity Press, 2016), 48.

69. Nathan Eisenberg, interview by Grace Harris, Andrew McWhinney, and Josh Messite, *Negation Magazine*, May 2021, https://www.negationmag.com/articles/interview-with-nathan-eisenberg.

70. Candace Taylor, "Real-Estate Frenzy Overwhelms Small-Town America: 'I Came Home Crying,'" *The Wall Street Journal*, May 20, 2021, https://www.wsj.com/articles/real-estate-frenzy-overwhelms-small-town-america-i-came-home-crying-11621511972.

71. Jock Serong, "'Priced Out': How Covid's Work-From-Home Boom Is Squeezing Small Towns," *The Guardian*, October 2, 2021, https://www.theguardian.com/australia-news/2021/oct/03/priced-out-how-covids-work-from-home-boom-is-squeezing-small-towns.

72. J.K. Dineen, "People Are Leaving S.F., But Not for Austin or Miami. USPS Data Shows Where They Went," *San Francisco Chronicle*, February 16, 2021, https://www.sfchronicle.com/bayarea/article/People-are-leaving-S-F-but-not-for-Austin-or-15955527.php.

73. Caitlin Harrington, "The Great Tech Exodus Didn't Quite Happen," *Wired*, March 8, 2022, https://www.wired.com/story/pandemic-remote-working-fail.

74. Daniel Oberhaus, "How Smaller Cities Are Trying to Plug America's Brain Drain," *Wired*, August 12, 2019, https://www.wired.com/story/how-smaller-cities-trying-plug-brain-drain.

75. Anthony P. Carnevale, Tamara Jayasundera, and Artem Gulish, *Good Jobs Are Back: College Graduates Are First in Line*, Georgetown University Center on Education and the Workforce, 2015, https://cew.georgetown.edu/cew-reports/goodjobsareback; Shoshana Zuboff, *The Age of Surveillance Capitalism: The Fight for a Human Future at the New Frontier of Power* (New York: PublicAffairs, 2019), 181.

76. Stephen Stock, Mark Villarreal, Sean Myers, and Kevin Nious, "Who Owns Silicon Valley: Stanford?" *NBC Bay Area*, November 1, 2019, https://www.nbcbayarea.com/news/local/who-owns-silicon-valley-stanford/2061716.

77. Landscape & Grounds, Sustainable Stanford (website), accessed August 12, 2022, https://sustainable.stanford.edu/landscape-grounds.

78. Marisa Kendall, "The Stanford Empire: The University Is More Than a Prestigious Place to Get A Degree," *The Mercury News*, November 4, 2019, https://extras.mercurynews.com/whoowns/stanford.html.

79. Stanford Facts, Stanford University, accessed February 22, 2022, https://facts.stanford.edu/administration/finances.

80. The Upshot, "Economic Diversity and Student Outcomes at Stanford University," *The New York Times*, accessed February 22, 2022, https://www.nytimes.com/interactive/projects/college-mobility/stanford-university.

81. National Research Council (US) Committee on Computing in the 21st Century, "Annex A—Stanford and Silicon Valley," in *Best Practice in State and Regional Innovation Initiatives*, ed. C.W. Wessner (Washington, DC: National Academies Press, 2013).

82. Ken Auletta, "Get Rich U.," *New Yorker*, April 23, 2012, https://www.newyorker.com/magazine/2012/04/30/get-rich-u.

83. Georgia Perry, "Silicon Valley's College-Consultant Industry," *The Atlantic*, December 9, 2015.

84. Diana Kapp, "Why are Palo Alto's Kids Killing Themselves?" *San Francisco Magazine*, May 18, 2015, https://www.sfgate.com/bayarea/article/Why-are-Palo-Alto-s-kids-killing-themselves-6270854.php; Jacqueline Lee, "Palo Alto: Cameras to Do Suicide Watch Along Train Tracks," *The Mercury News*, July 5, 2017, https://www.mercurynews.com/2017/07/05/palo-alto-cameras-to-do-suicide-watch-along-train-tracks.

85. Carolyn Walworth, "Paly School Board Rep: 'The Sorrows of Young Palo Altans,'" *Palo Alto Online*, March 25, 2015, https://www.paloaltoonline.com/news/2015/03/25/guest-opinion-the-sorrows-of-young-palo-altans.

86. Kapp, "Why Are Palo Alto's Kids Killing Themselves?"

87. Kate Santich, "Parramore Residents Struggle with Skyrocketing Rents As Revitalization Takes Shape," *Orlando Sentinel*, May 23, 2019, https://www.orlandosentinel.com/news/orange-county/os-ne-parramore-rents-rise-as-creative-village-grows-20190523-vjeskhsgjjc37gpqdlqermmaci-story.html.

88. Jim Saksa, "As Drexel Transforms University City, Communities Nearby Prepare for Gentrification," *WHYY*, July 13, 2018, https://whyy.org/segments/as-drexel-transforms-university-city-communities-nearby-prepare-for-gentrification.

89. Henry Grabar, "City Planning 101," *Slate*, May 11, 2018, https://slate.com/business/2018/05/universities-like-harvard-and-yale-are-real-estate-titans-too.html.

IV. TERROR

1. Sharon Noguchi, "Classrooms Are So Hot, Kids Turn Into 'Melted Cheese' in Alum Rock," *The Mercury News*, May 27, 2017, https://www.mercurynews.com/2017/05/27/classrooms-are-so-hot-kids-turn-into-melted-cheese-in-alum-rock.

2. Michelle Chen, "Silicon Valley Has a Homelessness Crisis," *The Nation*, March 30, 2017, https://www.thenation.com/article/archive/silicon-valley-has-a-homelessness-crisis.

3. San José Anti-Displacement Policy Network Team, *Ending Displacement in San Jose: Community Strategy Report,* January 2020, 17, https://www.sanjose ca.gov/home/showpublisheddocument?id=54715.

4. Tim Fang, "San Jose Home Buyers Need 22 Years to Save For Down Payment," *CBS San Francisco,* October 23, 2018, https://www.cbsnews.com/ sanfrancisco/news/san-jose-22-years-save-down-payment-zillow.

5. George Avalos, "Google downtown village plan gets its first OK from San Jose City Council," *The Mercury News,* June 20, 2017, https://www .mercurynews.com/2017/06/20/google-san-jose-negotiate-transit-village -downtown.

6. George Avalos, "Google Downtown San Jose Village Study Group Launches with Lively Discussion," *The Mercury News,* February 28, 2018, https://www .mercurynews.com/2018/02/28/google-downtown-san-jose-village-study -group-launches-lively-discussion-abobe.

7. Katherine Nasol, "Op-Ed: Why We Disrupted the Diridon Station Advisory Meeting," *San Jose Inside,* May 28, 2018, https://www.sanjoseinside.com/ opinion/op-ed-why-we-disrupted-the-diridon-station-advisory-meeting.

8. Amanda del Castillo, "San Jose City Council unanimously approves Google land plan," *ABC 7,* December 5, 2018, https://abc7news.com/google-san-jose -protest-land-sale/4837183.

9. Manfred B. Steger, *Globalization: A Very Short Introduction* (Oxford: Oxford University Press, 2003), 99–101; Elite universities similarly profess shock when their campus expansions displace families, though they also tout the sophistication of their social science departments.

10. Ingrid Burrington, "Who Gets to Live in Silicon Valley?" *The Atlantic,* June 25, 2018, https://www.theatlantic.com/technology/archive/2018/06/who -gets-to-live-in-silicon-valley/563543.

11. Chris Smith, "Bill de Blasio's Towering Problem," *New York Magazine,* June 28, 2013, https://nymag.com/news/politics/citypolitic/bill-de-blasio -2013-7; Javier C. Hernández, "A Mayoral Hopeful Now, de Blasio Was Once a Young Leftist," *The New York Times,* September 22, 2013, https://www .nytimes.com/2013/09/23/nyregion/a-mayoral-hopeful-now-de-blasio -was-once-a-young-leftist.html.

12. Sarah DeSouza, "Coming to a City Near You: de Blasio's Gentrification," *Columbia Political Review,* May 10, 2019, http://www.cpreview.org/ blog/2019/5/coming-to-a-city-near-you-de-blasios-gentrification.

13. Greenwich Village Society for Historical Preservation, *The Many Ways de Blasio's SoHo/NoHo Plan Encourages Developers to Build Without ANY Affordable Housing,* May 2021, https://media.villagepreservation.org/ wp-content/uploads/2021/05/14222415/Report-Many-Ways-de-Blasios -SoHo-NoHo-Plan.pdf.

14. Sara Dorn, "New York City Housing Advocates 'Extremely Disappointed' by Eric Adams' Budget," *City & State New York*, February 18, 2022; Emma Bowman, "NYC Homeless Advocates Say Mayor Eric Adams' Street Sweeps Aren't Working," *NPR*, May 13, 2022, https://www.npr.org/2022 /05/13/1097528966/nyc-eric-adams-homeless-sweeps.

15. City of Austin Anti-Displacement Task Force, *Recommendations for Action*, November 2018, https://www.austintexas.gov/sites/default/files/files/ Housing/Anti-Displacement_Task_Force_Final_Recommendations_ and_Report.pdf.

16. Ben Tobin, "Apple Announces Plan to Build $1 Billion Campus in Austin," *USA Today*, December 13, 2018, https://www.usatoday.com/story/tech/ 2018/12/13/apple-announces-plan-1-billion-campus-texas/229829600.

17. Daniel González, in discussion with the author, September 2020.

18. Stein, *Capital City*, 54, 58; Candace Jackson, "What Is Redlining?" *New York Times*, August 17, 2021, https://www.nytimes.com/2021/08/17/realestate/ what-is-redlining.html.

19. Austin—Gentrification and Displacement, Urban Displacement Project (website), accessed November 3, 2022, https://www.urbandisplacement .org/maps/austin-gentrification-and-displacement.

20. Earnie Young, "The Issues That Can Divide a Changing Neighborhood," *The Philadelphia Inquirer*, October 23, 2014, https://www.inquirer.com/news/ inq/changing-philadelphia-20141023.html.

21. Carol Lloyd, "A Blight on Urban Renewal / Are Bay Area Cities Abusing Eminent Domain as a Redevelopment Tool?" *SFGate*, March 4, 2005, https: //www.sfgate.com/entertainment/article/A-Blight-on-Urban-Renewal -Are-Bay-Area-cities-2726261.php.

22. Lees, Shin, and López-Morales, *Planetary Gentrification*, 109.

23. Vasudha, in discussion with the author, September 2021.

24. Jenna, in discussion with the author, September 2021.

25. Emily Green, "S.F. Mayor Ed Lee's Career Arc From Activist To Politician," *San Francisco Chronicle*, November 18, 2015, https://www.sfchronicle.com/ bayarea/article/S-F-Mayor-Ed-Lee-s-career-arc-from-activist-to-6599763 .php.

26. Sandy Perry, in discussion with the author, June 2021.

27. David Carbajal Torres, in discussion with the author, October 2021.

28. Austin Long, *Doctrine of Eternal Recurrence: The U.S. Military and Counterin-surgency Doctrine, 1960–1970 and 2003–2006* (Santa Monica: RAND Corpo-ration, 2008), 5.

29. Stanley Karnow, *Vietnam: A History* (New York: Penguin Books, 1985), 255; "[The people] may be likened to water and [the guerrillas] to the fish who inhabit it. . . . It is only undisciplined troops who make the people their

enemies and who, like the fish out of its native element, cannot live." Mao Tse-Tung, *Mao Tse-Tung on Guerrilla Warfare*, trans. Samuel B. Griffith (Washington, DC: U.S. Marine Corps, 1989), 93.

30.   William Rosenau, "'Our Ghettos, Too, Need a Lansdale': American Counter-Insurgency Abroad and at Home in the Vietnam Era," in *The New Counter-Insurgency Era in Critical Perspective*, ed. David Martin Jones, Celeste Ward Gventer, and M.L.R. Smith (London: Palgrave Macmillan, 2014), 116.

31.   Mike Davis, *Planet of Slums* (London: Verso Books, 2007), 109.

32.   Yulanda Ward, "Spatial Deconcentration in D.C.," *Midnight Notes* 2, no. 2 (July 1981).

33.   Jennifer S. Light, *From Warfare to Welfare: Defense Intellectuals and Urban Problems in Cold War America* (Baltimore: The Johns Hopkins University Press, 2003), 4, 62.

34.   David Galula, *Counterinsurgency Warfare: Theory and Practice* (Westport: Praeger Security International, 2006), 54.

35.   Galula, *Counterinsurgency Warfare*, 45.

36.   Galula, *Counterinsurgency Warfare*, 72.

37.   Sal Pizarro, "Google Gives $500,000 to Support Somos Mayfair Project," *The Mercury News*, May 18, 2017, https://www.mercurynews.com/2017/05/18/pizarro-google-gives-500000-to-support-somos-mayfair-project.

38.   Carolina Moreno, "Google.org Invests $1 Million to Help Create 'Latino Non-Profit Accelerator,'" *Huffington Post*, August 25, 2017, https://www.huffpost.com/entry/googleorg-invests-1-million-to-help-create-first-latino-non-profit-accelerator_n_59a02536e4b06d67e33721e8.

39.   George Avalos, "Google Grants and Volunteers Tackle Homelessness, Bolster Job-Seeking Skills," *The Mercury News*, November 29, 2018, https://www.mercurynews.com/2018/11/29/google-grants-and-volunteers-tackle-homelessness-bolster-job-seeking-skills.

40.   Sandy Perry, in discussion with the author, June 2021.

41.   Jennifer Elias, "Google's Plans for a Mega-Campus in San Jose Lurk Behind Its Recent $1 Billion Housing Pledge," *CNBC*, July 11, 2019, https://www.cnbc.com/2019/07/11/google-san-jose-expansion-helped-drive-1-billion-housing-pledge.html.

42.   Vicente Vera, "San Jose-Google Benefits Fund Could Take 10 Years to Pay Out," *San José Spotlight*, May 25, 2021, https://sanjosespotlight.com/san-jose-google-benefits-fund-could-take-10-years-to-pay-out.

43.   "Local activists protest new Google development in front San Jose conference," *ABC* 7, July 10, 2018, https://abc7news.com/google-development-san-jose-protest-protesters-silicon-valley-rising/3738759.

44.   Unlike similarly named organizations, Serve the People San José was not a

front group for the short-lived sect of Sendero Luminoso aficionados calling themselves the Red Guards.

45. Jeff Spross, "Can Silicon Valley Help Expand the Middle Class?" *The Week*, March 6, 2015, https://theweek.com/articles/542540/silicon-valley-help-expand-middle-class.

46. Kyle Martin, "New Report: Google Campus Will Lead to $235M More in Rent Spikes," *San José Spotlight*, June 12, 2019, https://sanjosespotlight.com/new-report-google-campus-will-lead-to-235m-more-in-rent-spikes.

47. George Avalos, "Community Groups Issue Demands to Google Over Downtown San Jose Village," *The Mercury News*, April 12, 2018, https://www.mercurynews.com/2018/04/12/community-groups-issue-google-downtown-san-jose-village-demands.

48. D, in discussion with the author, July 2022.

49. Inderjeet Parmar and Imran Choudhury, "Black Lives Matter Must Avoid Being Co-Opted by American Corporate Philanthropy," *The Conversation*, July 15, 2020, https://theconversation.com/black-lives-matter-must-avoid-being-co-opted-by-american-corporate-philanthropy-141927.

50. Jennifer Elias, "How Google Won Over Some of Its Biggest Critics to Build a Mega Campus In San Jose," *CNBC*, June 27, 2021, https://www.cnbc.com/2021/06/27/how-google-won-over-biggest-critics-of-san-jose-mega campus.html.

51. Sam Bloch, "'Overworked and Underpaid': Google's Cafeteria Workers Form a Union," *The Counter*, January 7, 2020, https://thecounter.org/googles-cafeteria-workers-union-silicon-valley; Madeline Stone, "22 Mouthwatering Pictures of Google's Legendary Free Food," *Business Insider*, October 6, 2014, https://www.businessinsider.com/photos-free-food-google-cafeteria-2016-9.

52. Google, 2021 Diversity Annual Report, https://about.google/belonging/diversity-annual-report/2021.

53. Héctor Tobar, "Viva Gentrification!" *New York Times*, March 21, 2015, https://www.nytimes.com/2015/03/22/opinion/sunday/viva-gentrification.html.

54. Robert L. Allen, *Black Awakening in Capitalist America: An Analytic History* (Trenton: Africa World Press, 1990), 144, 149.

55. Allen, *Black Awakening*, 231.

56. Allen, *Black Awakening*, 225.

57. Allen, *Black Awakening*, 163–164.

58. Allen, *Black Awakening*, 239.

59. Report of The National Advisory Commission on Civil Disorders, Appendix J: Special Interim Recommendations of the Commission, February 29, 1968, 318, https://belonging.berkeley.edu/sites/default/files/kerner_commission_full_report.pdf.

60. Phillip M. Bailey and Tessa Duvall, "Breonna Taylor Warrant Connected to Louisville Gentrification Plan, Lawyers Say," *Louisville Courier Journal*, July 5, 2020, https://www.courier-journal.com/story/news/crime/2020/07/05/lawyers-breonna-taylor-case-connected-gentrification-plan/5381352002.

61. Jason Laughlin, "In a Plan for a Safer, Vibrant 52nd Street, Worried West Philly Neighbors See Gentrification Looming," *The Philadelphia Inquirer*, February 21, 2020, https://www.inquirer.com/news/west-philadelphia-gentrification-52nd-street-redevelopment-20200221.html.

62. Robert Klemko, "After Walter Wallace Is Fatally Shot by Police, A Friend Contemplates How to Release the Anger," *The Washington Post*, November 1, 2020, https://www.washingtonpost.com/national/after-walter-wallace-is-fatally-shot-by-police-a-friend-contemplates-how-to-release-the-anger/2020/11/01/1e030812-1ad1-11eb-82db-60b15c874105_story.html.

63. Louis Lin, "'Order Maintenance' Policing and Its Role in Gentrification," Economic Opportunity Institute, August 29, 2017, https://www.opportunityinstitute.org/blog/post/order-maintenance-policing-and-its-role-in-gentrification.

64. Lam Thuy Vo, "They Played Dominoes Outside Their Apartment for Decades. Then the White People Moved in And Police Started Showing Up," *BuzzFeed News*, June 29, 2018, https://www.buzzfeednews.com/article/lamvo/gentrification-complaints-311-new-york.

65. Davis, *Planet of Slums*, 33.

66. Tom Gissler and Laura Thompson, "The Cop Who Quit Instead of Helping to Gentrify Atlanta," *Mother Jones*, September 14, 2020, https://www.motherjones.com/crime-justice/2020/09/the-cop-who-quit-instead-of-helping-to-gentrify-atlanta.

67. Vasudha, in discussion with the author, September 2021.

68. Jazmyn Henderson, in discussion with the author, September 2021.

69. David Carbajal Torres, in discussion with the author, October 2021.

70. John Spencer, "The City is the Battlefield of the Future," *The Wall Street Journal*, July 19, 2017, https://www.wsj.com/articles/the-city-is-the-battlefield-of-the-future-1500500905.

71. Akil Vicks, "Atlanta Is Building a "Cop City" on the Site of a Former Prison Farm," *Jacobin*, July 12, 2022, https://jacobin.com/2022/07/atlana-cop-city-south-river-forest; Jennifer Bamberg, "Controversial West Side Cop Academy Will Have Mock Neighborhood For Training. Here's What It Will Look Like," *Block Club Chicago*, August 10, 2022, https://blockclubchicago.org/2022/08/10/controversial-west-side-cop-academy-will-have-mock-neighborhood-for-training-heres-what-it-will-look-like.

72. Colonel Marc Harris et al., *Megacities and the United States Army: Preparing*

for a Complex and Uncertain Future, Chief of Staff of the Army, Strategic Studies Group (June 2014), 5, 12, https://api.army.mil/e2/c/downloads/351235. pdf.

73. Ananya Roy et al., *(Dis)Placement: The Fight for Housing and Community After Echo Park Lake*, UCLA Luskin Institute on Inequality and Democracy (2022), 101, https://challengeinequality.luskin.ucla.edu/2022/03/23/displacement.

74. Roy et al., *(Dis)Placement*, 129.

75. Roy et al., *(Dis)Placement*, 23.

76. Luz Pena, "Tenderloin Residents Plead for Help After Nonprofit Worker Meant to Keep Streets Safe Shot in SF," *ABC 7*, March 24, 2022, https://abc7news.com/tenderloin-district-san-francisco-sf-shooting/11593874.

77. "How to Fight the Google-Campus: A Proposal," *Shitstorm: Anarchistische Zeitung* vol. 2 (January 2018), https://theanarchistlibrary.org/library/anonymous-how-to-fight-the-google-campus.

78. "Woman's Google Glass Attack in SF Bar Spurs Huge Social Media Backlash," *CBS News Bay Area*, February 26, 2014, https://www.cbsnews.com/sanfrancisco/news/google-glass-attack-against-social-media-consultant-spurs-huge-backlash.

79. Bobby Allyn, "Point Breeze Developer Claims Arson Is Part of Backpack Against Gentrification," *WHYY*, May 3, 2017, https://whyy.org/articles/point-breeze-developer-claims-arson-is-part-of-backlash-against-gentrification.

80. David Chang and Dan Stamm, "'Anarchists' Damage High-End Cars, Newly Developed Properties in Philly, Leave Behind Anti-Gentrification Message," *NBC Philadelphia*, May 2, 2017.

81. "With this in mind, the typical popular gathering in Germany, at which workers calmly hear speakers out over a pint of beer to make themselves conscious of the goals and program of Social Democracy, is an act no less revolutionary than the last collective uprising in Moscow." Rosa Luxemburg, "Rosa Luxemburg's 'The Tactics of Revolution,'" trans. Joseph Muller, *Jacobin*, March 32, 2021, https://jacobin.com/2021/03/rosa-luxemburg-tactics-of-revolution.

82. Cory Sharber, "City Council Members Call for Extension of UC Townhomes HUD Contract," *WHYY*, September 8, 2022, https://whyy.org/articles/university-city-townhomes-protest-resident-demands-outside-philadelphia-city-hall.

83. Class war is sometimes used as a synonym for revolution, a state of affairs to be brought about or avoided. The revolutionary would advocate for this sort of war just as the neoconservative advocates for his war in the foothills of Caracas. In fact, the English term comes from early translations of the

Communist Manifesto's opening line: "The history of hitherto existing society is the history of class struggles." This war is of a different sort: not a future occurrence but an enduring reality.

84. Michel Foucault, *Society Must Be Defended: Lectures at the Cóllege de France 1975–76*, ed. Mauro Bertani and Alessandro Fortana, trans. David Macey (New York: Picador, 2003), 15–16.

V. WAR

1. "A Thousand Li," *Chuǎng* 1 (2016), https://chuangcn.org/journal/one/a-thousand-li.

2. Estelle Sommeiller and Mark Price, *The New Gilded Age: Income inequality in the U.S. by state, metropolitan area, and county*, Economic Policy Institute (2018), https://www.epi.org/publication/the-new-gilded-age-income-inequality-in-the-u-s-by-state-metropolitan-area-and-county.

3. Kenny Stancil, "Socialism is Gaining Popularity, Poll Shows," *Truthout*, June 26, 2021, https://truthout.org/articles/socialism-is-gaining-popularity-poll-shows.

4. Google, 2021 Diversity Annual Report, 41, https://about.google/belonging/diversity-annual-report/2021.

5. Olúfẹ́mi O. Táíwò, "Identity Politics and Elite Capture," *Boston Review*, May 7, 2020, https://www.bostonreview.net/articles/olufemi-o-taiwo-identity-politics-and-elite-capture.

6. Statewide Strike Support Organizing Committee, San Francisco State Strike Mass Convergence flier, SF State College Strike collection, San Francisco State University, accessed August 17, 2022, https://diva.sfsu.edu/collections/strike/bundles/237237.

7. Third World Liberation Front, No Deals—Fight Against Racism for Self-Determination—Grant the 15 Demands for TWLF Now!, SF State College Strike collection, San Francisco State University, accessed August 17, 2022, https://diva.sfsu.edu/collections/strike/bundles/187974.

8. Tanya Schevitz, "S.F. State to Mark 40th Anniversary of Strike," *SFGate*, October 26, 2008, https://www.sfgate.com/bayarea/article/S-F-State-to-mark-40th-anniversary-of-strike-3264418.php.

9. George Mason Murray Press Conference, SF State College Strike collection, San Francisco State University, retrieved August 17, 2022, https://diva.sfsu.edu/collections/sfbatv/bundles/187251.

10. Sheryl Sandberg and Nell Scovell, *Lean In: Women, Work, and the Will to Lead* (New York: Alfred A. Knopf, 2013), 8–11.

11. Táíwò, "Identity Politics and Elite Capture."

12. Emerald, in discussion with the author, October 2021.

13. George Avalos, "Google's Javier Gonzalez: Google village should be

'anchored in San Jose's culture,'" *The Mercury News*, https://www.mercury news.com/2018/04/19/sv-chat-javier-gonzalez-google.

14. Daniel González, in discussion with the author, September 2020.

15. Kate Aronoff, "Are the Democratic Socialists of America for Real?" *The New Republic*, August 7, 2017, https://newrepublic.com/article/144229/ democratic-socialists-america-real.

16. Jim Creegan, "The Left Wing of the Permissible: The Politics of Michael Harrington," *CounterPunch*, September 7, 2017, https://www.counterpunch .org/2017/09/07/the-left-wing-of-the-permissible-the-politics-of-michael -harrington; Maurice Isserman, "Remembering Michael Harrington, A Heroic Democratic Socialist Leader," *In These Times*, July 31, 2015, https:// inthesetimes.com/article/michael-harrington. Though Harrington cri- tiqued the anti-democratic personality cults of Stalinist bureaucracies, such critique must not have extended to the scrupulously democratic organiza- tion he alone was continually elected to lead.

17. John Nichols, "Bernie Sanders: 'I Am Prepared to Run for President of the United States,'" *The Nation*, March 6, 2014, https://www.thenation.com/ article/archive/bernie-sanders-i-am-prepared-run-president-united-states -updated-march-19.

18. Alexandria Ocasio-Cortez, *60 Minutes*, CBS News, January 6, 2019, https:// www.cbsnews.com/news/more-from-rep-alexandria-ocasio-cortez-on-60 -minutes.

19. Nik Brandal, Øivind Bratberg, and Dag Einar Thorsen, *The Nordic Model of Social Democracy* (London: Palgrave Macmillan, 2013), 9.

20. The Thom Hartman Program Daily Take Team, "The United States Needs to Realize FDR's Dream and Adopt the 'Nordic Model,'" *Truthout*, May 16, 2016, https://truthout.org/articles/the-united-states-needs-to-adopt-the -nordic-model.

21. Friends of Bernie Sanders, "Health Care as a Human Right—Medicare for All," BernieSanders.com, retrieved July 1, 2022, https://berniesanders.com/ issues/medicare-for-all.

22. David Redvaldsen, "Labour movement in the Nordic countries," nor- dics.info, February 19, 2019, https://nordics.info/show/artikel/labour -movement.

23. Nik Brandal et al., *Nordic Model of Social Democracy*, 34, 39.

24. J. Robert Constantine, "Eugene V. Debs: an American paradox," *Monthly Labor Review* (August 1991): 31, https://www.bls.gov/opub/mlr/1991/08/ art4full.pdf.

25. Nima Sanandaji, "Nordic Countries Aren't Actually Socialist," *Foreign Pol- icy*, October 27, 2021, https://foreignpolicy.com/2021/10/27/nordic-coun- tries-not-socialist-denmark-norway-sweden-centrist.

26. Hettie O'Brien, "If You Think Denmark Is All Borgen and Social Equality, Take a Look at Its Awful 'Ghetto' Law," *The Guardian*, June 27, 2022, https://www.theguardian.com/commentisfree/2022/jun/27/denmark-ghetto-law-eviction-non-western-residents-housing-estates.

27. Heather Farmbrough, "Copenhagen Startups Need to Think Global Earlier," *Forbes*, October 18, 2019, https://www.forbes.com/sites/heatherfarmbrough/2019/10/18/copenhagen-startups-need-to-think-global-earlier.

28. Redvaldsen, "Labour Movement in the Nordic Countries."

29. George Lakey, "Labor Lessons from Scandinavia," *Democratic Left*, December 4, 2017, https://www.dsausa.org/democratic-left/labor_lessons_from_scandinavia.

30. Lois Werner, "West Virginia's Strike Is No 'Wildcat,'" *New Politics*, March 4, 2018, https://newpol.org/west-virginia-strike-no-wildcat.

31. Michael Harrington's framing for organizing within the Democratic Party. See Maurice Isserman, *The Other American: The Life of Michael Harrington* (New York: PublicAffairs, 2000), 301.

32. Albert Goldman, *What is Socialism? Three Lectures for Workers* (New York: Pioneer Publishers, 1938), 39; Sam Marcy, "The Global Class War and the Destiny of American Labor," May 20, 1953, https://www.marxists.org/history/etol/writers/marcy/gclasswar/1953_Global_Class_War.html. *Workers World*, from which the PSL split well after the end of the Soviet Union, was unique in supporting both sides of the conflict between China and the USSR, holding that both nonetheless remained in the socialist camp.

33. Rebecca Fannin, "China to US Tech Investment Plunges 79% To Lowest Level in 7 Years Amid DC Crackdown," *Forbes*, January 21, 2019, https://www.forbes.com/sites/rebeccafannin/2019/01/21/china-to-us-tech-investment-plunges-79-to-lowest-level-in-7-years-amid-dc-crackdown.

34. TRIUM Global Executive MBA (website), accessed July 1, 2022, https://www.triumemba.org.

35. Deirdre Griswold, "Why the Imperialists Hate Huawei," *Workers World*, May 30, 2019, https://www.workers.org/2019/05/42449.

36. Ryan Hass et al., "U.S.-China Technology Competition: A Brookings Global China Interview," *Brookings Institution*, December 23, 2021, https://www.brookings.edu/essay/u-s-china-technology-competition.

37. Mara Hvistendahl, "Oracle Boasted That Its Software Was Used Against U.S. Protesters. Then It Took the Tech to China," *The Intercept*, May 25, 2021, https://theintercept.com/2021/05/25/oracle-social-media-surveillance-protests-endeca.

38. V. I. Lenin, "Report on the Unity Congress of the R.S.D.L.P.: VII The End of the Congress," in *Lenin: Collected Works Volume 10*, trans. Andrew Rothstein (Moscow: Progress Publishers, 1978), 380.

39. Errico Malatesta, "The Dictatorship of the Proletariat and Anarchy," in *The Method of Freedom: An Errico Malatesta Reader*, ed. Davide Turcato, trans. Paul Sharkey (Oakland: AK Press, 2014).

40. V.I. Lenin, *What Is to Be Done?* (New York: International Publishers, 1929), 28, 79, 116, 124. For example: "[The] national tasks of Russian Social-Democracy are such as have never confronted any other Socialist party in the world. Farther on we shall deal with the political and organizational duties which the task of emancipating the whole people from the yoke of autocracy imposes upon us. At the moment, we wish merely to state that the *role of vanguard can be fulfilled only by a party that is guided by an advanced theory.*"

"The principal thing, of course, is *propaganda and agitation* among all strata of the people. The Western-European Social-Democrats find their work in this field facilitated by the calling of public meetings, to which *all* are free to go, and by the parliament, in which they speak to the representatives of *all* classes. We have neither a parliament, nor the freedom to call meetings, nevertheless we are able to arrange meetings of workers who desire to listen to *a Social-Democrat.*"

"[In] a country with a despotic government, the more we *restrict* the membership of this organization to persons who are engaged in revolutionary as a profession and who have been professionally trained in the art of combating the political police, the more difficult will it be to catch the organisation . . . [and] the *wider* will be the circle of men and women of the working class or of other classes of society able to join the movement and perform active work in it."

"But what takes place very largely automatically in a politically free country, must in Russia be done deliberately and systematically by our organizations. . . . As the spontaneous rise of the labouring masses becomes wider and deeper, it not only promotes from its ranks an increasing number of talented agitators, but also of organisers, propagandists, and 'practical workers'. . . . When we shall have detachments of specially trained working-class revolutionists who have gone through long years of preparation . . . no political police in the world will be able to contend against them."

41. The Second Congress of the Communist International in 1920 mandated that "parties belonging to the Communist International must be built up on the principle of democratic centralism . . . [with] iron discipline, bordering on military discipline." O. Piatnitsky, *The Twenty-One Conditions of Admission into the Communist International* (New York: Workers Library Publishers, 1934), 31.

42. Wendy Brown, *Walled States, Waning Sovereignty* (New York: Zone Books, 2014), 25.

43. Jodi Dean, "Neofeudalism: The End of Capitalism?" *Los Angeles Review of*

Books, May 12, 2020, https://lareviewofbooks.org/article/neofeudalism-the-end-of-capitalism.

44. Harris et al., *Megacities and the United States Army*, 15.

45. Perinaz Bhada, "The Global City Indicators Program: A More Credible Voice," *Directions in Urban Development* (June 2009), https://documents1.worldbank.org/curated/en/350011468337792616/pdf/491660BRI0City10Box338943B01PUBLIC1.pdf.

46. Parag Khanna, "How Much Economic Growth Comes from Our Cities?," *World Economic Forum*, April 13, 2016, https://www.weforum.org/agenda/2016/04/how-much-economic-growth-comes-from-our-cities.

47. *Power Shifts: A Decade of Extreme Consequences and Transformational Possibilities, Ten-Year Forecast 2019*, Institute for the Future, https://www.iftf.org/projects/ten-year-forecast-2019-power-shifts.

48. Riccardo Petrella, quoted in *The Global Trap: Globalization and the Assault on Prosperity and Democracy* by Hans-Peter Martin and Harald Schumann, trans. Patrick Camiller (London: Zed Books Ltd, 1997), 20.

49. Saskia Sassen, "Saskia Sassen on How The Powerless Can 'Hack' Global Cities," *The Architect's Newspaper*, August 10, 2017, https://www.archpaper.com/2017/08/saskia-sassen-hack-global-cities.

50. Sassen, "How the Powerless Can 'Hack' Global Cities."

51. Huey P. Newton, "Speech Delivered at Boston College: November 18, 1970," in *The Huey P. Newton Reader*, ed. David Hilliard and Donald Weise (New York: Seven Stories Press, 2002), 168.

52. "The Empire Is Trembling: Two Translations from the Uprising in Chile," trans. Ill Will Editions, *Liaisons*, October 22, 2019, https://en.liaisonshq.com/2019/10/22/the-empire-is-trembling.

53. Martin and Schumann, *The Global Trap*, 18.

54. Joe Frem, Vineet Rajadhyaksha, and Jonathan Woetzel, *Thriving Amid Turbulence: Imagining The Cities of the Future*, McKinsey & Company (2018), https://www.mckinsey.com/industries/public-and-social-sector/our-insights/thriving-amid-turbulence-imagining-the-cities-of-the-future.

55. Jonathan Andrews, "How Cities Can Stay Ahead of the Competition," *Cities Today*, July 2, 2016, https://cities-today.com/how-to-stay-ahead-of-the-competition.

56. Carlo Ratti, "We Need More Urban Innovation Projects Like the 'Google City.' This Is Why," *World Economic Forum*, September 23, 2020, https://www.weforum.org/agenda/2020/09/google-smart-cities-urban-innovation-technology.

57. Selma James, "Wageless of the World," in *Sex, Race, and Class—The Perspective of Winning: A Selection of Writings, 1952–2011* (Oakland: PM Press, 2012), 107.

58. Phil Neel, "New Battlefields," interview by e-Komite, *Ill Will*, June 30, 2022, https://illwill.com/new-battlefields.

59. Sandy Perry, in discussion with the author, June 2021.

60. Dezmond Goff, in discussion with the author, September 2020.

61. James, "Wageless of the World," 144; Calvin Welch, "Ed Lee's Development Legacy and The End of 'Balanced Growth,'" *48 Hills*, January 7, 2018, https://48hills.org/2018/01/ed-lees-record.

62. John W. Miller, "How Should Catholics Think About Gentrification? Pope Francis Has Some Ideas About Urban Planning," *America: The Jesuit Review of Faith & Culture*, November 1, 2021, https://www.americamagazine.org/politics-society/2021/11/01/gentrification-pittsburgh-moral-economy-241733.

63. Jorge Luis Borges, *Collected Fictions*, trans. Andrew Hurley (London: Penguin Books, 1998), 325.

64. Shoshana Zuboff, *The Age of Surveillance Capitalism: The Fight for a Human Future at the New Frontier of Power* (New York: PublicAffairs, 2018), 8.

65. Karl Marx, *Capital Vol. 1*, trans. Ben Fowkes (London: Penguin Books, 1990), 874.

66. Marx, *Capital Vol. 1*, 878, 915.

67. Peter Kropotkin, *The Conquest of Bread and Other Writings*, ed. Marshall Shatz (Cambridge: Cambridge University Press, 1995), 221.

68. Silvia Federici, *Caliban and the Witch* (Brooklyn: Autonomedia, 2004), 9.

69. "How To Fight the Google-Campus: A Proposal."

70. Paula Molina, "Jorge González de Los Prisioneros, Autor de 'El baile de los que sobran,' Himno de la Protesta en Chile: 'Es Muy Lindo, Pero Muy Triste Que Se Siga Cantando,'" *BBC News Mundo*, October 27, 2019, https://www.bbc.com/mundo/noticias-america-latina-50197900.

71. "El Baile de Los Que Sobran," track 3 on Los Prisioneros, *Pateando piedras*, EMI, 1986.

72. André Gorz, *Stategy for Labor: A Radical Proposal*, trans. Martin A. Nicolaus and Victoria Ortiz (Boston: Beacon Press, 1967), 8–9; Andrew Lee, "The Revolutionary Power of Abolitionist Demands," *ROAR Magazine*, October 15, 2020, https://roarmag.org/essays/revolutionary-potential-abolitionist-demands.

73. Martin and Schumann, *The Global Trap*, 1–5.

74. Martin and Schumann, *The Global Trap*, 1–5.

75. Erin McCormick, "The Daily Battle to Keep People Alive as Fentanyl Ravages San Francisco's Tenderloin," *The Guardian*, April 23, 2022, https://www.theguardian.com/us-news/2022/apr/23/san-francisco-homelessness-street-team-fentanyl.

76. World Bank, *World Development Report 2016: Digital Dividends* (Washington, DC: World Bank, 2016), 118, https://www.worldbank.org/en/publication/wdr2016.

77. DC Policy Center, *2018 State of the Business Report: Towards a More Inclusive Economy* (Washington, DC: DC Chamber of Commerce, 2018), 2, https://www.dcpolicycenter.org/publications/2018-state-of-the-business-report-towards-a-more-inclusive-economy.

78. Lyndsay Walsh, "How Can We Address Inequality in the Twenty-First Century? Start With Climate Change," *Finance & Development* 56, no. 4 (December 2019): 39–41, https://doi.org/10.5089/9781498316880.022.

79. Carrick Reddin, "Community Land Trusts: A Solution to the Global Housing Crisis," *World Economic Forum*, June 25, 2021, https://www.weforum.org/agenda/2021/06/community-land-trust-housing-access.

80. This is the implicit strategic objective of the popular movement against displacement.

81. Robert Graham, *We Do Not Fear Anarchy, We Invoke It: The First International and the Origins of the Anarchist Movement* (Oakland: AK Press, 2015), 28.

82. Graham, *We Do Not Fear Anarchy*, 55, 167.

83. Eric Thomas Chester, *The Wobblies in their Heyday: The Rise and Destruction of the Industrial Workers of the World during the World War I Era* (Santa Barbara: Praeger, 2014), vii.

84. Peter Marshall, *Demanding the Impossible: A History of Anarchism* (Oakland: PM Press, 2010), 502.

85. J. Sakai, "Beginner's Kata: Uncensored Stray Thoughts on Revolutionary Organization," Kersplebedeb, April 14, 2018, https://kersplebedeb.com/posts/kata/.

86. William C. Anderson and Zoé Samudzi, "The Anarchism of Blackness," *ROAR Magazine* 5 (Spring 2017): 74.

87. Emerald, in discussion with the author, October 2021.

Index

and transit-oriented develop-
ments, 35; turnover of, 81–82.
See also working class
Lugalia-Hollon, Ryan, 7
Luxemburg, Rosa, 189n81
luxury units, 67–69
Lyft, 137–38

Madison, WI, 69
Malatesta, Errico, 139
Manchester, UK, 80
Mao Zedong, 29–30
maps, 147, 148
marginalization, 156
Marx, Karl, 15, 80, 148, 155
Marxism, 137–39
mass resignation, 87
McNealy, Scott, 151–52
media, 55
Medicare for All, 134
memorials, 52, 54
Mexico, 29, 47, 52, 53
Meza, José, 44–45
migrant workers, 87
Mike Davis, 52
militancy, 150
military-industrial complex, 13,
63–64, 119
Miller, Jonathan, 87
Milwaukee, WI, 80
Minneapolis, MN, 69
Mission District, San Francisco,
56, 72
Moretti, Enrico, 20
mortgages, 8, 17
Moses, Robert, 6–7
Moskowitz, P. E., 10
Mural de la Raza (Meza), 44–45, 50
murals, 44–45, 50
Murray, George Mason, 128, 129

Nasol, Katherine, 100

National Guard, 116
nationalism, 28
nation-states, 28, 141. *See also* counterinsurgency
Navarro Gustavo, Bernal, 50
Neel, Phil, 145
neighborhood names, 56–58
neoliberalism, 8–9, 163n31
New Economy. *See* gentrification
economy
New York, NY: and Airbnb, 60;
Amazon campus, 149; and de
Blasio, 102–03; Harlem renam-
ing, 56–57; as modern city, 141;
and Moses, 6–7; park control,
56; tickets out of town, 63;
vacancies, 9
Newark, NJ, 116
Newton, Huey P., 142
Nextdoor (website), 3
Nightingale, Naomi, 41
Nixon, Richard, 116
non-disclosure agreements
(NDAs), 98, 99
nonprofits, 3–4, 110–12, 115–16
Northgate, 57
Not In My Backyard (NIMBY), 70

Oakland, CA, 13, 32, 57, 116
Oakwood, 41–43
Oakwood, Venice, 50
Occupy movement, 31, 32, 76
Office of Technology Licensing, 94
Oracle, 138
Orlando, FL, 95
outsourcing, 18, 20, 65

pacifism, 150
Packard Automotive Plant, 20–21
Palo Alto, CA, 94–95
Paris Commune, 16, 29, 80
Parsons, Lucy, 169n62

Party for Socialism and Liberation (PSL), 137, 138, 192n32
patriarchy, 78–79
Penske, Jay, 42, 43
Peraza, Bryan, 45, 46, 53
Perry, Sandy, 33, 65, 106, 110, 145
Peru, 118
Philadelphia, PA: arson and graffiti, 121; Black Bottom, 57–58, 95; businesses closing, 75, 77; Cafe Life unionizing, 76; Doctors' Row, 53; HIV and homelessness, 63; Kensington, 64–65; and police funding, 118; property taxes, 104; Temple stadium protest, 2; University of Pennsylvania, 57–59, 95
philanthropic co-optation, 110–13, 115–16
placation, 151–52
places, 39–40
police: and class, 3; and counterinsurgency, 106–10, 116, 119, 122; and displacement, 117–19; and highway protests, 36; in pre-revolutionary Russia, 139; at San José Google meetings, 100–01; training facility in Atlanta, 119; in Venice, 42. See also counterinsurgency
politics of representation, 126–27
poor people, 35, 109, 144, 145–46
power vs. representation, 129, 131–32
practical anarchism, 155–57
precarious tenants vs. unhoused, 64
precarious workers, 82–83
prisons, 7
privatization, 28, 61
production, 11, 15
professionals, 7, 10, 19, 26, 90–91. See also Google; Silicon Valley; tech workers

profit, 3–4, 10, 24–25
proletariats, 15. See also working class
property damage, 121
property taxes, 104
property values, 65
protests: affordable housing Philadelphia, 2; budget hotel in Rochester, 2; cities vs. suburbs, 144–46; direct action, 1–2, 121–22; Google campus in San José, 1; highways, 36; Occupy Wall Street, 31; paint on artwork in LA, 2; San José Google meetings, 100, 101; and space, 37; squatters in Berlin, 1; squatters in Philadelphia, 32; tech in San Francisco, 1–2; zoning in San Francisco, 67–68. See also revolts/rebellions; revolution
Protracted People's War, 30
Proudhon, Pierre-Joseph, 154
public transit, 24, 34–36
punks, 26, 155

Qilombo, 32
queer people, 127, 131

racial capitalism, 8
racism, 4, 7–8, 88, 181n65. See also redlining
RAND Corporation, 109
Ratti, Carlo, 143
redlining, 4, 103–04
reforms, 150
remote work, 91–92
renaming areas, 56–58
rent parties, 48
rentals: and Airbnb, 60; in Barcelona, 59; and Great Recession, 8, 163n26; luxury units,

67–69; precarious tenants vs.
unhoused, 64; in San José, 18,
111; YIMBY's ideas, 67–68
representation, 128, 129–32. *See also*
identity politics
resignations, 82, 87
revolts/rebellions, 15–16, 29–30, 79,
80, 144, 150. *See also* counterinsurgency; protests
revolution: and Black Power, 116,
142; and class war, 189–90n83;
and membership to Social-
Democracy, 193n40; and
militancy, 122; and propagation of ideas, 79; syndicalist
view of, 86, 180n55; and typical
workers' gatherings, 189n81
Rifkin, Jeremy, 151
Roberts, Julia, 42
Rochester, NY, 2
Rosdail, Jennifer, 56
Rosenthal, Tracy, 71
Roy, Rustum, 151–2
Russia, 134, 139, 155, 192n32,
193nn40–1
Rust Belt, 20

Sakai, J., 155
salaries, 18, 19, 94, 178n38
San Francisco Bay Area, 13–14, 35,
97. *See also specific areas*
San Francisco, CA: condo construction, 9; evictions, 60;
homelessness, 63; Mission
District, 56, 72; tech shuttle
blockades, 1–2; Tech Workers
Coalition, 72; workers leaving,
91; zoning protests, 67–68
San Francisco State College, 128–29
San José, CA: overview, 17–18;
blighted land, 104; Google
campus in, 1–2, 98–101, 104–05,

110–13; highway protest, 36;
history of, 65; home down
payments, 98; homeless-
ness, 97; living standards,
18–19; Mural de la Raza, 44,
50; population decline, 14;
rent parties, 48; rental costs,
18; salaries in, 18, 19; school
funding, 97; Serve the People,
101, 111, 186–7n44. *See also* San
Francisco Bay Area; Silicon
Valley
Sandberg, Sheryl, 130
Sanders, Bernie, 133
Santa Ana, CA, 45, 53, 63, 70, 118–19
Santa Clara county, 17–18
Santa Mari la Juarica, 47
Santiago, Chile, 35–36
Sassen, Saskia, 141–42
Save Venice, 42–43
Savings & Loan Crisis, 7–8
Scandinavian socialism, 134, 135
Schwab, Klaus, 81
Scott, James C., 55
Seattle, WA, 7, 83, 118
Second Congress of the Commu-
nist International, 193n41
Second Industrial Revolution, 81
segregation, 115
Seigal, Lenny, 94
Serve the People San José, 101, 111,
186–7n44
service jobs, 80
Session, Noni, 51
Shenzhen economic zone, 87–88
Sidewalk Labs, 21–22
Silicon Valley, 1–2, 13, 14, 22, 93–94.
See also Google; San José, CA;
tech industry; tech workers
Silicon Valley Rising (SVR), 110–11
skills, 166n22
slavery, 8

Institute for Anarchist Studies

The Institute for Anarchist Studies (IAS) was founded in 1996 and seeks to further antiauthoritarian thought by supporting the work of radical writers, filmmakers, and podcasters. We offer editorial mentorship, working closely with new and established writers to develop their ideas and voices for a general audience, as well as online and print publication opportunities: our website and social media presence; our annual journal, *Perspectives on Anarchist Theory*; and our various book series (published in partnership with AK Press). We also sponsor speakers, performances, and theory tracks at conferences and other public events. We fund leftist thinkers and culture makers, and prioritize creators of minority identities and those who operate outside of academia and therefore have less access to intellectual or material resources. When possible, we give grants to promote work that could not otherwise be made.

For more about the IAS, visit: anarchiststudies.org.

AK PRESS is small, in terms of staff and resources, but we also manage to be one of the world's most productive anarchist publishing houses. We publish close to twenty books every year, and distribute thousands of other titles published by like-minded independent presses and projects from around the globe. We're entirely worker run and democratically managed. We operate without a corporate structure—no boss, no managers, no bullshit.

The **FRIENDS OF AK PRESS** program is a way you can directly contribute to the continued existence of AK Press, and ensure that we're able to keep publishing books like this one! Friends pay $25 a month directly into our publishing account ($30 for Canada, $35 for international), and receive a copy of every book AK Press publishes for the duration of their membership! Friends also receive a discount on anything they order from our website or buy at a table: 50% on AK titles, and 30% on everything else. We have a Friends of AK ebook program as well: $15 a month gets you an electronic copy of every book we publish for the duration of your membership. *You can even sponsor a very discounted membership for someone in prison.*

Email **friendsofak@akpress.org** for more info, or visit the website: **https://www.akpress.org/friends.html**.

There are always great book projects in the works—so sign up now to become a Friend of AK Press, and let the presses roll!